ETERNITY IS WORTH GETTING RIGHT

Reasoning Together about God, Religion, and Reaching Heaven

Patrick J. O'Bryan

THIRD EDITION
(First edition titled: In the Beginning)
(Second edition titled: Eternity is Worth Getting Right)

Library of Congress Cataloging-in-Publication Data

ISBN-13: 9780615270197
ISBN-10: 06152701911

O'Bryan, Patrick J. (Patrick Joseph)
Eternity Is Worth Getting Right: Reasoning Together about God, Religion, and Reaching Heaven / Patrick J. O'Bryan.
Includes bibliographical references and appendices.

Cover design by author
(earth and moon superimposed over star field).
Cover graphics by Pacesetter Printing, Princeton, KY.
Space photographs courtesy of NASA
(National Aeronautics and Space Administration).

Total pages: 104
Text software: Microsoft Word 2003.

Printed in the United States of America

CONTENTS

FOREWORD

As the cover says, I'm just a common man with no formal education in theology or religion. Just consider me a rank amateur-- like most people are.

Nevertheless, regarding God, religion, and spiritual matters, this common man is 100 percent sure of one thing - Eternity has always been in my heart! Isn't that true for you? Don't we all at least occasionally think about what's going to be in store for us after our life on this earth is finished?

And doesn't almost everyone have hope in something concerning their eternal place in the cosmos? You may presume you will go to heaven because you were born into some religion and baptized, or some preacher, priest, or friend tells you that you'll get there. Or you may have grown up and selected one of the world's many spiritual beliefs that appeals to you and claims to possess the right way to heaven.

Wouldn't it be nice to have great peace of mind in knowing for sure that you're on the true road to heaven? Don't you agree with me that eternity is worth getting right? A friend of mine once said, "An unexamined faith is not worth having."

Well, a big reason I wrote this little book is so you can spend just a few hours of your time with me in a simple, common-sensed reasoning journey where we reason *together* about our prospects for eternity. We'll go from considering whether heaven might even exist to distinguishing the true way to get there.

So, I humbly invite you to come along with me on this journey. We're going to see many interesting and amazing sights along the way. I can't wait to get started!

INTRODUCTION

You and I will begin this reasoning journey *together* in Chapter 1. But first, let's consider a few thoughts about our reasoning that show us *why* we can expect it to lead us where we want to go, namely to successfully distinguish the ultimate truth of how we can get our eternity right--by reaching heaven.

We know that each of the major religions of the world claims to possess the truth of "who God is" and how we can gain salvation into his eternal heaven. We see a large assortment of salvation beliefs, ranging from the various beliefs of many organized religions to atheism (there is no god).

And this assortment of salvation beliefs continues to grow. The two most popular new salvation beliefs are "religious pluralism" and "universalism" (as they are called by those who keep up with and write about spiritual beliefs in the world today). Most people living under religious pluralism or universalism are unaware that their beliefs have been named.

Religious pluralism says "all paths (religious salvation beliefs) lead to heaven." Many religious leaders and preachers accept religious pluralism as valid. Religious pluralism presumes that God is rather easy going, and he accepts the salvation beliefs of all religions. Pluralism says that no religion is superior to another, and no religion has the right to proclaim itself right or true and the others false--or even inferior. Pluralism is so popular today that many people in an organized religion no longer rely on the sacred written text(s) of that religion for the basis of their salvation belief. Or, they accept the written word of their religion regarding salvation, but not all of it.

Universalism says that "all people go to heaven" no matter what they *sincerely* believe, even if they believe there is no god. Universalism appeals to people because it suggests that God accepts everyone's 'sincere' personal beliefs regarding salvation, especially that they are free to live by their own moral standard and God will still welcome them into heaven.

Well, let's you and I consider the following simple and profound thought: Suppose God is a loving God who just happens to be quite particular about who he accepts into *his* heaven, based on one's willingness to follow *his* direction for reaching heaven. Doesn't that idea seem possible, even reasonable? Could it be taking a huge gamble with one's eternity to presume that God is so carefree about his heaven that he accepts man's ways to get there?

But, if God truly cares about us, isn't it also reasonable to expect he would communicate with us in some way to make it clear to us exactly how we can get our eternity right--so we don't miss out on heaven? Wouldn't a loving God let us know whether or not he accepts the beliefs that "all paths lead to heaven," or "everyone goes to heaven"?

And isn't it reasonable to expect that the true God who made the universe would communicate his requirement for reaching heaven in a way that is fairly simple to distinguish as coming only from him, and not made up by man? Wouldn't this be true no matter what form of communication he might extend toward us?

Finally, we should set some guidelines to follow in our reasoning so we proceed in a fair, orderly, and timely path toward our goal. How about we agree to reason together without any spiritual biases--including the bias, or belief, that God even exists? To help us at being unbiased, we will start our reasoning by trying to get ourselves into a humble state of mind. And lastly, we plan to keep our reasoning simple.

Chapter 1
A Humble Beginning

Remember, here we shall reason together in search of the truth of how we can get our eternity right, meaning we want to learn precisely *how* we can know for sure that we will go to heaven when we die.

Now, let's start our reasoning with a few simple questions and thoughts for us to ponder: If there were a dozen gods out there, or even just two, then would there really be any *true* God at all? If a person believes in God, isn't it their natural idea of God that he is, by definition, the creator and sustainer of all things? Doesn't it seem most reasonable that just one all-powerful God has always existed; and, in the beginning he made everything like he wanted? Think about it.

You know, of all the world's religions, Christianity is the best known and the most criticized when it comes to claiming to possess the only true way to heaven! Christians call their God the "creator God." The Bible begins with the words, **"In the beginning God made the heavens and the earth"** (Genesis 1:1). That's Genesis, Chapter 1, verse 1. Christians claim that Christianity is the only religion or faith that was actually started by this creator God! And they say the Bible was written by men with divine inspiration from this God's Holy Spirit. They say the Bible contains not a single error! Well, with all these claims, how on earth can Christians explain the fact that Jesus Christ said (in the Bible) that many people who claim to know him and proclaim his name will not be in heaven? Perhaps many people who think they are Christian ought to consider that there just might be more to reaching heaven ("getting saved") than *thinking* you're a Christian!

The point is, our eternity is worth getting right. It saddens me to see so many people gambling so frivolously with their eternity by not taking a little time to examine their salvation beliefs to make darn

sure they are aligned with the truth, but some people do.
Sir Winston Churchill said:

> "Truth is incontrovertible.
> Panic may resent it;
> ignorance may deride it;
> malice may distort it;
> but there it is."
>
> Appendix 4, ref.2

Let's end this first chapter with this important thought: It is generally accepted that one of the most beneficial principles anyone can apply in life is to be humble, especially when first taking on some new endeavor. We see this in business, in making friendships, and even in sports. Surely you agree that having some humility is generally good for all of us. So I respectfully ask you to stay with me as we continue our reasoning by spending a few moments looking at some *humbling* facts, questions, ideas and such. I think you will find these things very interesting and enjoyable to consider.

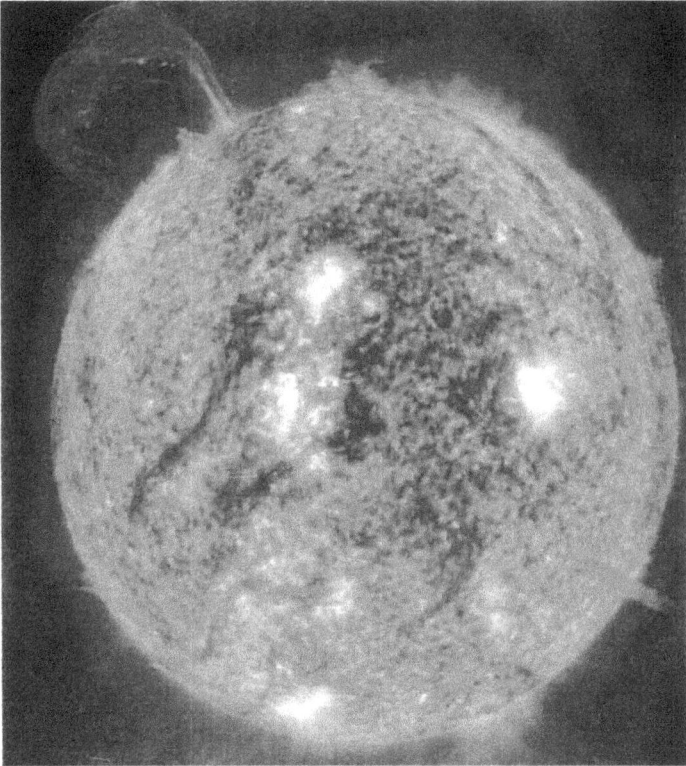

Space photos are courtesy of NASA
(National Aeronautics and Space Administration).

The earth's sun is one of 100 billion stars in our own Milky Way galaxy. Our sun is 864,000 miles across and burns at a rate of 5 million tons per second, producing 513 trillion horsepower (513,000,000,000,000hp) of energy per second! How many years has the sun been doing this?

As suns go, our sun is average size.

The earth's moon is 240,000 miles from us. The moon provides us light during the night. Gravity between the earth and the moon causes the tides which clean the oceans along their boundaries with the continents. Also, scientists say the moon's gravity helps keep the earth's rotation from wobbling out of control! And the earth's gravity is *just* strong enough that the moon does not fall to the earth or fly away from it! Do you suppose all this is a coincidence?

Saturn is the second largest planet in our solar system (Jupiter is the largest). Saturn's rings are 150,000 miles wide and only .6 mile thick. The rings are made up of tiny ice fragments and some rocks.

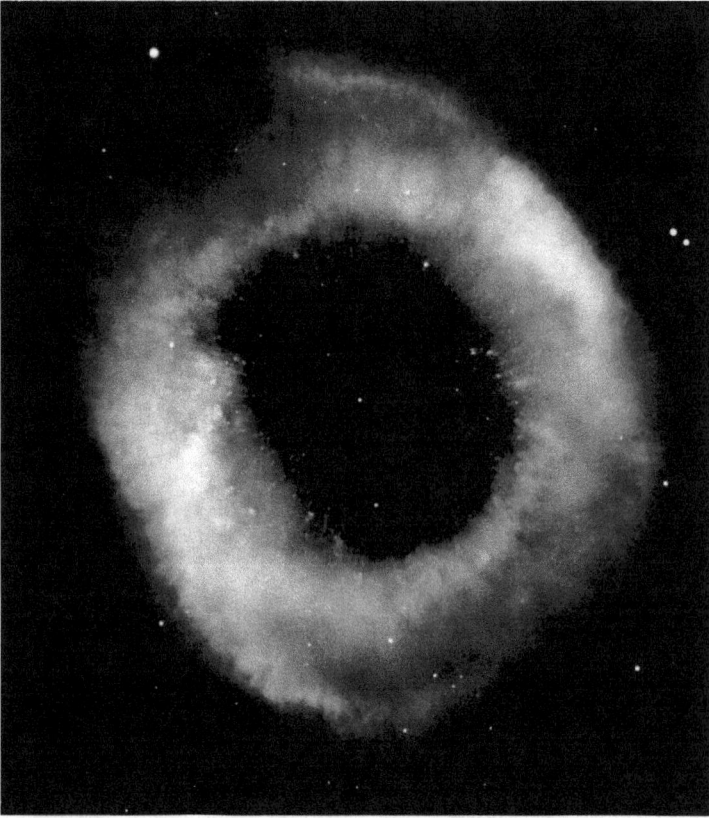

Helix Nebula is a trillion mile wide barrel of gas left over from an exploding star. This nebula is 450 light years from us. Telescopes have found a wide assortment of space nebulas of different types and appearance.

A "light year" is the *distance* light travels in one year, moving at its speed of 186,000 miles per second! So a light year works out to be a distance of 5.9 trillion miles!

M81, a spiral galaxy, is 12 million light years from us. This extravagant light show is caused by the emitting of light from massive short-lived stars and other stars bunching together.

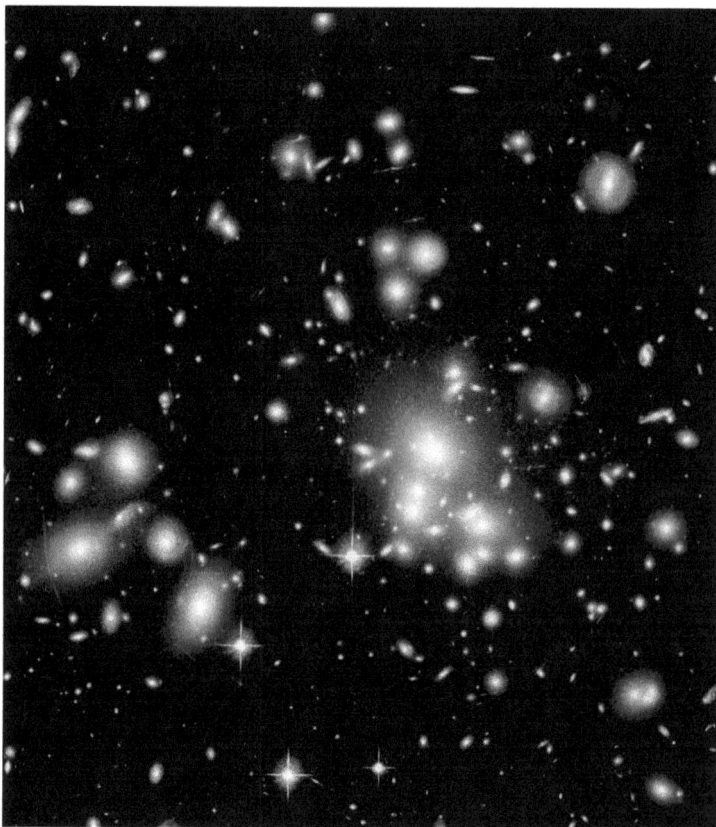

Abell 1689 is a cluster of hundreds of galaxies crowded by trillions of stars. It is 2.2 billion light years away from us. This place is so massive it visibly warps space! Light from more distant objects is bent as it travels through the cluster. This is called gravitational lensing.

The Hubble Ultra Deep Field is 13 billion light years away. These are some of the most distant galaxies known. This field is home to 10,000 galaxies! Astronomers estimate there are a billion trillion stars in what they have seen *so far* of the universe! And they say they've only had time to point their telescopes toward a small portion of the universe that is in the visible range of the newest more powerful telescopes.

Chapter 2
How Smart Are We?

Let's continue our little exercise in humility. Do you think you have most things in life all figured out? Man is at the top of the food chain right--so why shouldn't we think we have life figured out? Look at all the wonderful advances man has made in recent decades in science, electronics, medicine, and many other things. When we watch TV or read the newspaper we are constantly reminded of man's genius and creativity. Has all this made us so proud that we're tempted to believe we know everything--including everything spiritual?

Does any of this sound familiar in your life?

Please understand, I don't want to hurt your feelings or make you angry. Rather, I just want you to sit back and consider with me for a moment this one *humbling* thought: If there is a God who made the universe, then how smart could we actually be--compared to him?

I've learned the hard way that I need to keep working at being humble, or that mean ole pride comes back and hurts me. Perhaps we all need a slice of "humble pie" once in a while.

Chapter 3
A Slice of Humble Pie

Now let's look at some additional humbling questions or thoughts. I call this having a slice of humble pie. You know, humble pie might not taste sweet to us, but it certainly is good for us. We sure can't say humble pie is fattening.

1. Does the universe full of galaxies have a physical boundary or end?

2. If the universe does end, then what's on the other side of it? Is the whole universe enclosed in some kind of bubble? Could there be many universes?

3. What holds the universe in place?

4. What is gravity? Isaac Newton quantified gravity with an equation (Newton's Law); but even the brilliant Newton admitted he did not know what gravity actually is. And we still don't know all that much about gravity. Other than calling it a force, what is gravity? And why is it there?

5. What is time? If you were somehow put in charge of time, could you stop time tomorrow at noon? Did time have a beginning? Will time end someday?

6. What is light? Where did light *first* come from?

7. How come light travels at 186,000 miles per second (the "speed of light") everywhere in the known universe--and not say 190,000 miles per second?

8. Scientists say they know the "chemicals of life;" and they give us numerous theories on how life began. So, how come no human being has ever made one thing come alive? It seems like almost every day scientists tell us some new theory on how the chemicals of life first came together, and "voila," life was there! So, why can't scientists create life in a lab? No person has ever made anything come to life--ever!

9. If man evolved from the ape, how come we haven't found the remains of creatures between the ape and man? Sure, living things do evolve, or change characteristics over time. To a limited extent, we can even manipulate or nudge nature to evolve, as we have done with our breeding of dogs. But come on, let's be honest here. Isn't it a huge stretch of the imagination to say that the incredibly 'well designed' human body and mind evolved from a puddle of chemicals struck by lightning--or whatever? There is no hard evidence for anything like that, is there?

10. We know from physics experiments that a typical atom, the building block of all matter, is a mere three hundred millionths of an inch across! And amazingly, every atom is made up of even much smaller particles. The atom's nucleus is composed of positively charged particles called protons and neutrally charged particles called neutrons. Orbiting around this nucleus are negatively charged particles called electrons. Physicists say the attraction force between protons and electrons is what holds the atom together. Atoms combine to form molecules of matter.

Looks like man has the atom all figured out doesn't it. Wrong! I believe it's fair to say that scientists acknowledge there is far more that we don't know about the atom, and all matter, than what we do know. Recently for example, more particles inside the atom ("sub-atomic" particles) have been discovered. It's like the building blocks of all the material in the universe are little universes in themselves--full of endless amazing and unknown things!

11. And how come everything in the universe just happens to abide by the uniform laws of physics that we know, apparently without exception?

Like many people, I think it is reasonable to acknowledge that these things, and many others, are only a tiny smattering of the things God created in the beginning that man knows so little about. We could go on and on here, couldn't we? Thomas Edison said, "We don't know one millionth of one percent about anything." You and I can't even begin to comprehend the vastness of God's knowledge and power! Compared to God, we know so little--and can do only such little things.

Considering the universe's obvious complex *design*, Albert Einstein made his famous statement, "If there is a watch, there is a watch maker." Einstein was acknowledging that obviously this "watch maker" is God.

There's an old saying that goes something like this: "Sometimes I sit and think - sometimes I just sit." We are thinking now.

What is all the cosmos for? What do you suppose is our true position in the cosmos? Where do you think you'll be a thousand years from now? What if there is a God who knows you and I exist, and even knows what we're thinking right now?

Chapter 4
Eternity

What if there really is an eternity? And what if it is true that each one of us will actually spend eternity in either heaven or hell?

Here's a neat way to sort of relate to eternity. Consider that each year of your life is like a grain of sand. Thus, a hundred years' worth of living would be equivalent to about a match head's volume of sand.

Now, consider the vastly innumerable grains of sand all around the world. That would be just too many grains of sand to ever fathom! And yet, if we counted every grain of sand on earth as a year, they all would still only add up to a mere glimpse of eternity! Eternity has no end!

The older I get the faster life seems to go by and the shorter my whole life seems to be. The Bible compares our relatively short lifetime on earth to a **"mist that appears for a little while and then vanishes"** (James 14:4).

What if our life after that short-lived "mist" does continue somehow and someplace for all eternity? Now that's something to think about. Perhaps we should take very seriously the idea that eternity is worth getting right.

Chapter 5
Where Did the Universe Come From?

Common sense and science both point to a beginning to everything. Most scientists agree that the ongoing expanding and aging universe clearly suggests it had a definite beginning from a specific time and place. They call this beginning the "big bang." But many of these scientists have a difficult time accounting for the 'initial' existence of all matter and energy in the universe--as do strict evolutionists. Atheists generally rely on the difficult theory that everything just always existed.

Most people already agree that a creator God must exist, just as the great genius Albert Einstein believed. Isn't it unreasonable not to believe in such a God, when we take a moment to consider the wonders of the universe and the magnificent earth with all its living things?

Don't we all naturally seem to have thoughts of a creator God when we gaze up at the stars at night, stand beside a beautiful flowing stream in the countryside, look up at a majestic mountain, calmly admire a beautiful sunset, or watch and enjoy the earth's wondrous animals, birds, and fishes?

I can't help believing that God made the universe--including all the galaxies of stars and planets spread out with seemingly no end. I believe God made everything we see through the Hubble Space Telescope. We've seen that the first verse of the Bible says, **"In the beginning God made the heavens and the earth"** (Genesis 1:1).

Could we all be *made* with a natural longing to know God and a desire to reach heaven? The Bible answers this question in Romans 1:20 where Paul says, **"For since the creation of the world God's invisible qualities--his eternal power and divine nature--have been clearly seen, being understood from what has been made, so that men are without excuse."** And Ecclesiastes 3:11 says, "He (God) **has also set eternity in the hearts of men.**" No matter how you or I view the Bible, aren't these verses at least intriguing to ponder?

To me, it just takes a little humility and common sense to acknowledge that - of course God made the universe. There's that humility thing again.

Nevertheless, perhaps you don't believe in God, or you don't believe he created the universe. Maybe you believe in science, or evolution, or something else, as the basis for all existence, and even as the basis for what you believe you will experience after your life on earth is over. If that's how you feel, then the things you will be seeing and considering as we reason onward will likely be especially interesting and surprising to you.

Chapter 6
Heaven and Hell

A popular rock song some years ago exclaimed: "I swear there ain't no heaven and I pray there ain't no hell." What is the actual truth about all these things--heaven, hell, religion, salvation and such? The truth just has to be there doesn't it? I know one thing for certain; if my eternal salvation depends on being on the right side of this truth, then that's exactly where I want to be. Don't you?

Remember, we talked earlier about how easy it is for us to think we have everything in life all figured out? Well, many people say they have figured out that since they are generally nice to others, do all sorts of good deeds, and don't kill or steal, there's just no way that a good god would exclude them from heaven. It's a fact; many people appear to be banking their eternal salvation on their *feelings* that a good god would not send good people to hell. What do you think?

And then there are people these days who say, "I'm not concerned about heaven, hell, or religion; and I would prefer not to talk about them." These people generally do not watch television shows centered around religion, and they are hesitant to even pick up a book like this one you're now holding.

Perhaps, for the moment, we ought to just recognize the fact that all human beings seem to naturally have thoughts about life after death-- including heaven and hell. Could we be made that way, by design?

Chapter 7
God Must be Sovereign

If you can agree with me that it's rational to acknowledge that God made everything, then isn't it logical to say he thought it all up and made it all just like he wanted? And, if God made everything, then clearly everything is his! The earth is his and the universe is his. So, isn't it accurate to say that even though we live on the earth, we don't own it - God does?

If such a creator God owns everything, then obviously he has the total right to do just as he pleases with *his* creation. This is called God's "sovereignty."

Many people, even some who say they believe in a single creator God, just cannot accept the sovereignty of God. It's as if they're too proud to recognize and concede that any other being could be at a higher level or "position in the cosmos" than they. What good is it to believe in God if one cannot humble oneself and admit God's absolute superiority?

Yes, if there is a creator God, then common sense tells us he is sovereign. What are the ramifications (results) of God's sovereignty? We'll talk more about this in the next chapter.

Chapter 8
Ramifications

Now, let's reason about this: When a believer in God accepts that God is sovereign, then the great ramifications of God's sovereignty naturally become so apparent.

The God of the Bible says he is sovereign. He declares to all people through the words of the prophet Isaiah: **"My purpose will stand, and I will do all that I please"** (Isaiah 46:10).

The Bible says this about God: **"God, the blessed and only Ruler, the King of kings, and Lord of lords, who alone is immortal and who lives in unapproachable light, whom no one has seen or can see. To Him be honor and might forever, Amen"** (1 Timothy 6:15-16).

Here are three profound thoughts we surely ought to include in our reasoning here: First, the sovereign God could make a heaven and hell if he chooses. Second, he can make the final rules for admission into *his* heaven--presuming he made a heaven. And third, the sovereign creator God, whoever he may be, can set the absolute standards for good and evil. Aren't these ideas sensible?

In light of these things, isn't it wise for a person to consider and investigate the possible existence of a 'single' sovereign God--and his way to heaven - *before* choosing to follow some other way to heaven that man has thought up?

Chapter 9
If God is Good...

Let's think for a moment about something important and utterly crucial. If there is a single sovereign God, and if he is good, wouldn't he do certain things for us--his creation? If this God is good, and he has made a heaven and a hell, wouldn't he want us to know about them? Wouldn't he communicate with us in some way to show us how to reach heaven and how to avoid hell? Wouldn't he provide a way that you and I may know the truth about these places he made? And wouldn't he give us a way to know him personally right now?

If this God showed us his way to heaven, and told us his way is the *only* way that is acceptable, would that make him mean or cruel, or just the one in charge? That's a humbling thought, isn't it?

It seems obvious to me that a God who would create the universe, give me life, and offer me the opportunity to live with him in heaven for all eternity must be a good God! As the saying goes, "That's a no-brainer."

Chapter 10
What Really Matters

Sure, we can reason sound things about how a good God would watch out for us.

Could the one true creator God have already revealed and proven his goodness to all mankind? Regarding this, we know there are a number of so-called sacred religious texts that claim to be the authentic, revealed word of the one true God. For centuries, the Bible has been the one such text which is the one most known worldwide, the one most talked about, and the one most scrutinized.

The point is, if we want to make sure we *can* get our eternity right, isn't it smart for us to first see which, if any, of these sacred religious texts stands out from the rest as the only one that is clearly the word of the one true creator God? For God's word to stand out like this, there would have to be things so special and so unique about it that the only way to account for these great things is to attribute them to God. What really matters is that we base our hope for getting our eternity right on the *right* written word, presuming there is one!

Surely God did not intend for us all to have a PhD in theology. Therefore, isn't it sound logic to expect that the 'true' word of God was written so common people like you and I would be able to make just a basic examination of it and recognize it as his.

You know, most people appear totally committed to their religious and spiritual beliefs; however very few people have made any real examination of their beliefs or the written word, if any, that forms the basis for their beliefs.

Chapter 11
Christian Claims about the Bible

Christians tell us that the Bible not only claims to be the error free word of the one true God, it backs up that claim! They say the Bible is packed with evidence of its own truthfulness by the complete accuracy of its entire text--especially its accounts from ancient history and its hundreds of fulfilled prophecies. Christians say the Bible's *self-contained* and verifiable evidence is what distinguishes it from all the other sacred texts of other world religions or beliefs.

Christians claim the Bible was written by divine inspiration from the one true God through his Holy Spirit! They are convinced God inspired the writers of the Bible to say exactly what he wanted said, from the first word of Genesis to the last word of Revelation. They also say that God tells us, in the Bible, precisely how we can get our eternity right by securing our eternal place with him in heaven and never lose it.

Not to be swayed by all this impressive Bible talk from Christians, you may be like many who think the Bible is just a nice book about how to live a particular kind of moral life, but is still just another book written by men.

You know, it is undisputed that the Bible is the best selling and the most widely distributed book of all time. And, Christianity, as defined by the Bible, is the one religious belief that all other beliefs are most commonly compared to--all over the world.

Here's another way of looking at all this: If we wanted to debunk the idea that the one true God is communicating to us through some sacred book, wouldn't the Bible logically be the first book we would want to discredit? In the next chapter we will consider some amazing things that would have to be true if the Bible is true.

Chapter 12
If the Bible is True...

Let's continue our reasoning by answering the question, "What if the Bible is true?" Common sense tells us that if the Bible is true, then it has to be what it says it is - the authentic and error-free word of the one and only creator God who made the universe! As we shall see later on here, the Bible itself says it is *all* inspired by God. So, if the Bible is true, then there cannot be a single error in its entire text, no errors of history or prophecy or anything!

If the Bible is true, then there really is a heaven made by the God of the Bible. If the Bible is true, then we human beings were made by this God--in his image, so we look something like him. If the Bible is true, then Jesus Christ is who he said he is, namely, the Son of God or God in the flesh - God incarnate! Or, simply put, Jesus Christ is God. If the Bible is true, then Jesus truly was born of a virgin, Mary, just as portrayed in Christian celebrations of Christmas. If the Bible is true, then Jesus was killed by crucifixion and rose again after three days--proving his power over death! The "resurrection" of Jesus Christ is at the heart of the Christian faith. Without it, Christianity is fundamentally irrelevant.

And if the Bible is true, then (as it claims) there is only one way for anyone to reach heaven. If the Bible is true, then most people, including many who claim to be a Christian, are not on the road to heaven because they are banking their eternal salvation on things not seen in the Bible!

Let's think for a moment. If the old Bible is actually the word of the one true God, then shouldn't we see that - if we spend some time looking into the Bible and examining it? On the other hand, if the Bible is not the word of the one true God, shouldn't we see that, too? Wouldn't it be full of inaccuracies, errors, and inconsistencies relating to all sorts of things, particularly its hundreds of predictions or prophecies?

A Short Timeout

Let's recall the goal of our reasoning journey. Here's the gist of it: We're trying to see if we can use common sense reasoning to show us the true way of getting our eternity right. We're on this reasoning journey because something inside us tells us that eternity is worth getting right.

So far, we've looked briefly (and mostly in general terms) at the beliefs of Christianity, pluralism, and universalism. Don't you agree that we've reached the point in our reasoning where we are compelled by common sense to go ahead and find out for ourselves, once and for all, whether the Bible actually *is* the word of the one true God?

Let's look at some little known but 'crucial' things *in* the Bible and some not well known facts *about* the Bible that should help us rationalize for ourselves whether the Bible really matters, and whether the God of the Bible really matters. Most of the things we'll see will probably be totally new to you. Some are even unknown by many Christians. I think you'll find this part of our journey to be very interesting and different.

As you recall, we began our reasoning journey by working on our humility. Let's start this next leg of our journey with a little exercise aimed at reaffirming the great importance of humility in our search for finding how we can get our eternity right. In the next chapter, we'll consider what may be the most humbling fact that mankind could ever ponder--namely, our "position in the cosmos."

OK, time back in.

Chapter 13
Our Position in the Cosmos

Now, I respectfully ask you to consider, for a moment, the story of Job from the Bible, because Job's story is simply the best example I know of for 'how' we can know our true position in the cosmos. We don't have to believe the Bible to appreciate the lesson of Job's story. You've probably already heard something about it.

In the Bible, we see that Job had everything in life--a family, great wealth, and friends. Then he lost it all! He even lost his good health and was living in constant, extreme pain.

Understandably, Job was distressed about his troubled life. Then, Job was given the unique opportunity to question God directly concerning his troubles. Responding to Job, God asked, **"Where were you when I laid the earth's foundation?"** (Job 38:4). God and Job's conversation continued for a good while. Job learned so much from God, but everything he learned was *first* based on his own humility, which God helped him find.

You see, God simply explained to Job his true "position in the cosmos." He reminded Job that he was not around when God created the universe. God explained to Job that the universe and everything in it was made by God and belonged to God. God showed Job that Job's position in the cosmos was obviously far beneath God's position! Job learned that even his own existence was a gift from God. And Job learned that God owed him nothing.

Now, I respectfully take us go back to what God asked Job, and apply it to ourselves. Where were we in the beginning, when God laid the earth's foundation? Did we help God in his creating? Did God call on us to help design the earth and all its living things? Did he need our help in designing and creating the sun, the earth, the moon, the other planets in our solar system, and all the universe?

If you read the story of Job in the Bible, you will see God's great love for Job; and best of all, the story has a happy ending. Job found a great personal relationship with God, and God blessed him abundantly for the rest of his life!

So, have you ever seriously thought about what is your true position in the cosmos? I think about my true position in the cosmos all the time. I know it helps me to not loose sight of the things that really matter in life.

Chapter 14
The Frank Harbor Story

I met Dr. Frank Harbor in 1999 at his crusade for Jesus Christ, held in Elizabethtown, Kentucky. When I met Frank, he had just completed writing a book he titled *Reasons for Believing.*

Dr. Harbor is a very intelligent man. Not many years ago he was a sincere atheist who wanted to confirm the foolishness of any religion! So he set about doing extensive research of the world's religions. He considered things that are crucial to the integrity of any world religion: the historical and geographical accuracy of its sacred text(s), fulfillment of its written prophecies, supporting archeological discoveries and known scientific facts, common sense reasoning, and more.

His goal of showing all religions to be man-made, and therefore of no *eternal* value, was proceeding well - until he began examining Christianity. Dr. Harbor says, to his surprise, investigating Christianity caused him to see the Bible's amazing accuracy and truthfulness, and the unique hope of the Christian faith. He soon became a Christian; and he really got fired up for Jesus Christ. He wasted no time in completing his Ph.D. from The Southwestern Baptist Theological Seminary. He then took up defending Christianity in public by speaking and debating non-Christians in forums such as colleges, universities and such.

What a turnaround! Dr. Harbor even decided to write his book *Reasons for Believing*, where he describes his examination of Christianity, and shows the reader the things he found to be true about the Bible, Jesus Christ, and Christianity.

It seems reasonable to me that Dr. Harbor's story is at least some evidence that the Bible could be true and accurate. And, it also seems reasonable that we consider that this former skeptic's conversion story is not unusual at all. It is well known that many who put the religions of the world through such a rigorous examination, come away with the same conclusion Dr. Harbor did - namely that evidence is there to show Christianity is based on truth.

Note:

Many books like Dr. Harbor's *Reasons for Believing* have been written. I refer to his book because it is easy to read and understand. I do this on my own initiative--receiving no compensation of any kind for doing so.

Chapter 15
Do Bible Prophecies Come True?

Like we talked about before, if the Bible is truly the word of this *one and only* creator God, as it claims, then there wouldn't be any errors in it, including errors of historical fact or prophecy!

So then, aren't we compelled now in our reasoning to take a brief look at the prophecies and other facts in the Bible? This should be a good way we can examine the Bible to help us form an overall judgment about its truthfulness.

So we shall spend a little while doing this. But don't think for a second that this might get boring. No way! This part of *Eternity Is Worth Getting Right* was fascinating for me to learn about and to write. I think you'll like it.

Abraham Lincoln is known to have said, "The Bible is God's greatest gift to mankind." The Bible contains over 2,000 prophecies about Jesus Christ and the course of events in the world! Bible prophecies are the recorded (written) predictions of future events, made by the Bible prophets. Now let's look at a few Bible prophecies.

Some 600 years before Jesus Christ was born, the Bible predicted he would be born in the city of Bethlehem (Micah 5:2). As an engineer, I know that the mathematical odds of getting this one prediction right, by chance, are remote. Jesus was born in Bethlehem while Mary and Joseph were there for a census.

Centuries before crucifixion was used as a means of execution, it was prophesied that Jesus would be executed by being brutally beaten and **"pierced in his hands and feet,"** just as was seen in the Roman crucifixions that would take place (Isaiah 52:14, Zechariah 12:10, Psalms 22:16-18). We should ponder over that prediction.

The resurrection of Jesus Christ after three days in the grave was prophesied many times in the Bible, including Jesus' own foretelling of his death by crucifixion and his resurrection in Matthew 26:2 and John 3:14. It is very interesting to me that secular history (history reported outside the Bible) clearly shows that Jesus Christ existed, that he claimed he was the Son of God, and that he was crucified. Moreover, secular history cannot disprove his resurrection, while the Bible contains *eye-witness* detailed written accounts from Jesus' apostles that he truly did rise from the dead--just as foretold. They describe a number of his post-resurrection appearances to themselves and to others; and on one occasion the apostle John describes Jesus' *resurrected* appearance to a crowd of over 500 people (1 Corinthians 15:6)! We'll see more about these "eyewitness" apostles and the resurrection of Jesus in Chapter 22.

The Bible predicts many things about the Christian faith which Jesus Christ began. Here are two such examples: Matthew reports that Jesus said his church would withstand all attempts by Satan to destroy it (Matthew 16:18). Jesus' Christian church and his word are still here 2,000 years later, having withstood numerous attempts to discredit Jesus and the Bible! We see these *failing* attempts continue unabated in our day.

And the prophet Isaiah predicted thousands of years ago that God would **"raise up"** those to spread the gospel of Jesus Christ to the very ends of the earth (Isaiah 49:6). Jesus said the same thing in Matthew 24:14. Missionaries are accomplishing this today. There is now a concerted world-wide Christian effort to preach the gospel of Jesus to all nations, including all ethnic people groups, not just all geographically recognized countries.

The Bible prophets predicted, in detail, the rise and fall of great cities and kingdoms of the world. Such events relating to Babylon, the Persian Empire, the Greek Empire, the Roman Empire, and others, were accurately predicted and described far in advance of their occurrences. The hundreds of Bible passages predicting these and other such great historical events are too many to show here, but we'll look at several of them. You know, for a long time, Bible skeptics have been trying to show that there are errors of history recorded in the Bible--especially prophetic history. Don't you suppose that if these Bible skeptics had legitimately succeeded at disproving any Bible history, you would have heard about it, over and over?

Here's another example of the Bible's remarkably accurate predicted history. Even though Jerusalem and the holy temple were still standing at the time, the Old Testament prophet Isaiah predicted the persecution of the Jews and the destruction of the holy temple and the city of Jerusalem (see Isaiah 3:8, Jeremiah 11:9, Micah 3:12). Amazingly, Isaiah even predicted that the temple would be rebuilt 70 years after its destruction, through the Persian king Cyrus. He made this prediction 150 years *before* king Cyrus was born (Isaiah 44:28). Wow!

Here are two more examples of Bible prophecies for civilizations and cities, which were proven accurate by recorded secular history:

The prophet Ezekiel boldly foretold the demise of the kingdom of Edom, in a detailed account given in Ezekiel 35:1-15, where he relays God's words toward Edom: **"I will make you desolate forever; your towns will not be inhabited. Then you will know that I am the Lord."** Sure enough, history proved Ezekiel's prophecy to be accurate.

The prophet Isaiah was certainly accurate when he foretold of God's judgment against the great city Babylon (Isaiah 13). He says in Isaiah 13:19-20: **"Babylon, the jewel of kingdoms, the glory of the Babylonian's pride, will be overthrown by God like Sodom and Gomorrah. She will never be inhabited or lived in through all generations..."** Just as Isaiah predicted, Babylon was utterly destroyed and was not rebuilt nor re-inhabited!

Similar amazing Bible prophecies were made and were fulfilled for the cities of Tyre (Ezekiel 26:7-21), Sidon (Ezekiel 28:22-23), and Nineveh (Nahum 1-3, Zephaniah 2:13), just to name a few more. Archeologists continue to find evidence that these cities *used to* exist, as has been documented in the many books about the fulfillment of hundreds of Bible prophecies regarding kingdoms, cities, peoples, and such. What we've seen here isn't even the tip of the iceberg on the subject!

Let me ask you, have you heard of the Dead Sea Scrolls? These are ancient hand-written cloth scrolls of *original* Bible texts, discovered in the mid 20th century in Middle East caves. Other than very minor unimportant differences in punctuation and the use of prepositions and such, the Dead Sea Scrolls very closely match the Bible used today! For this reason, many people believe the Dead Sea Scrolls are one of the greatest archeological discoveries ever--that corroborate the integrity of the Bible. Books on these scrolls are in bookstores today (Appendix 4).

I think it is reasonable for you and me to also consider that Bible prophecies are not so general or vague as to be easily forecast. But rather, the Bible prophets many times boldly included additional details in their predictions, such as names, specific time frames, and such. The Bible prophets wrote that they were merely servants of God, and they said (in their writings) that they were just writing as they were led by inspiration from God.

Isn't it true, that people marvel when TV shows describe a few things that non-Biblical, and so-called "gifted prophets" (such as Nostradamus, Jean Dixon and others) have predicted, that appear to have come true? And yet, all these 'outside the Bible' prophets generally make hundreds of predictions, but can only legitimately be credited with a few close guesses! Even the few predictions they appear to get right are almost always general or could have several meanings. The media never tells the whole story about these so-called gifted prophets.

There are over 8,300 verses of prophecy in the Bible. That's about 27% of the Bible! Without a doubt, Jesus Christ is the most important prophet in the Bible. Many of his prophecies relate to the "last days" (the days leading up to his prophesied return to the earth), the final judgment of all people, and heaven and hell. Jesus' prophecies are given to us in the gospels of Matthew, Mark, Luke and John, and in Acts (written by Luke).

Later in Chapter 17, you and I will consider some of the Bible's many "last days" prophecies.

Many Bible scholars have written books, and some appear on TV, to recount some of the Bible's many *fulfilled* prophecies relating to wars, battles, floods, droughts, famines, plagues, disease epidemics, and much more!

Referring to God's hand in prophetic Bible scripture, the prophet Isaiah wrote, **"Declare what is to be, present it--let them take counsel together. Who foretold this long ago, who declared it from the distant past? Was it not I, the Lord? And there is no god apart from me, a righteous God and savior; there is none but me"** (Isaiah 45:21).

Chapter 16
A Cut Above

Still, after nearly 2,000 years since it was written, it is well known that the Bible continues to be scrutinized far more than any other book ever written. Over the centuries, many people have died for having a Bible in their possession. And yet, the Bible continues to be the #1 best selling book in the world with over one million bought every year! The Bible has now been translated, at least in part, into about three thousand languages.

Shouldn't we consider this logical statement? If Bible prophecies, ancient history, or other facts given in the Bible were proven to be false, then the world today would be so different. Thomas Paine obviously thought the Bible was full of false things when he wrote in his book, *Age of Reason*:

> "Five years from now there will
> not be a Bible in America.
> I have gone through the Bible
> with an ax and cut down all its trees."

And shouldn't we consider where the world might be without the Bible? It's a fact that the fundamental laws of our country and most of the world were originally derived from the old moral standards found in the Bible. Most historians agree that the Bible had great influence in the placing of the words "IN GOD WE TRUST" on our money.

Remember, Christianity was founded by Jesus Christ. Jesus says in Matthew 24:35, **"Heaven and earth will pass away, but my words will never pass away."** And the Bible says, **"...the grass withers and the flowers fall, but the word of the Lord stands forever"** (1 Peter 1:25).

As we try to search out the truth about our eternity and the truth of how we can reach heaven, perhaps we're compelled to seriously consider this: When the sacred books of other religions are examined anything like the Bible has been examined, they all fall short in comparison to the Bible! The sacred books of other religions or beliefs are generally void of detailed prophecies, and they typically contain numerous unexplainable errors relating to persons, places, events, geography, and such.

And, did you know that the sacred books of the world's other religions do not tell the story of God and man all the way through the end of world history, at least not in detail like the Bible does? Their end of history predictions are, at best, general and vague compared to the Bible's.

It seems logical to me that all attempts to discredit the Bible must have ended in utter failure, or the Bible most likely would have long ago been relegated to just a nice book on moral living. Have you ever read or heard about a single Bible prophecy or Bible fact that has ever been legitimately proven false? I haven't. Paraphrasing from Thomas Paine, no Bible trees have been cut down; instead, the Bible appears to be a 'cut above' the rest!

In light of all these things, don't you agree that we should certainly at least recognize that Jesus Christ was accurate when he prophesied, over 2,000 years ago that his words would never pass away?

Next, we will look at the Bible's "last days" prophecies. Wait till you see this!

Chapter 17
The "Last Days"

The **"last days"** is what the Bible calls the whole period between Jesus Christ's first appearing on earth and his "Second Coming"--not merely the period right before his Second Coming. The Bible has many prophecies about these "last days," especially those days right before Jesus returns. Today, Christians call the period of time right before Jesus returns, the "end times." Jesus himself foretold much concerning events of these so-called end times. We see this in the Bible writings of Matthew and Luke.

Bible prophecies fascinate me. Let's take a look at some Bible prophecies about the last days, particularly the end times, to see whether these old prophecies, or predictions, were accurate. This should be interesting. Many Bible scholars believe we are in the end times period of the last days--right before Jesus' Second Coming.

Here's *some* of what Jesus foretold would be happening near the end of the last days--or what we call the end times? In Matthew 24:4-14, Jesus says, **"Watch out that no one deceives you. For many will come in my name, claiming, 'I am the Christ,' and will deceive many. You will hear of wars and rumors of wars, but see to it that you are not alarmed. Such things must happen, but the end is still to come. Nation will rise against nation, and kingdom against kingdom. There will be famines and earthquakes in various places. All these are the beginning of birth pains.**

Then you will be handed over to be persecuted and put to death, and you will be hated by all nations because of me. At that time many will turn away from the faith and will betray and hate each other, and many false prophets will appear and deceive many people. Because of the increase of wickedness, the love of most will grow cold, but he who stands firm to the end will be saved. And this gospel of the kingdom will be preached in the whole world as a testimony to all nations, and then the end will come." What a vivid description of our day by Jesus Christ--2,000 years ago!

You know, because we are now seeing a *concentration* of all these things, and more, that Jesus and the other prophets foretold in the Bible, it's no wonder many people believe we are living in the end times part of last days--close to Jesus' return. It's obvious that over the course of history we've always had such events happening. But, never before have they *all* been *increasing* together anything like today. These things are so prominent in the news nowadays, aren't they? The "increase" in these things is frequently reported and described in the media.

There are more wars now than ever in recorded history. Natural disasters like floods, droughts, earthquakes, hurricanes, and tornadoes are happening so often these days that we expect to see them occur someplace almost every day! And the United Nations reports that about 30,000 children die in the world every day due to famine related malnutrition, starvation, and disease. The AIDS virus continues taking lives by the millions. New potentially killer viruses are developing all the time, and scientists warn that some of these could also kill millions of people around the world.

Remember, Jesus prophesied that in the last days many false prophets would arise and **"deceive many"** (Matthew 24:4-5). Welcome to the modern world, where we see more and more of this sad fact. Simple reasoning strongly suggests there are many false prophets today. If there is only one true God, and he accepts only *his* way to reach heaven, then doesn't it follow that many of today's religious and spiritual teachers can only be false prophets? Perhaps we should also consider that starting a new religion appears to be as common today as starting a new type of business. What about truth?

And, we know about the growing hatred toward Christians. I recently learned that the Christian church now sadly reports that you and I are living in the period of history that is seeing the greatest number of Christian martyrs ever!

Here's an interesting last days prophecy. In Ezekiel 36:24-27 and Jeremiah 23:3-4, the Bible clearly foretold the migrating of the Jewish people from Israel to the far reaches of the world; and in the end times great numbers of them would return home to Israel. Well, they sure spread throughout the nations of the world didn't they-- even to the USA and Russia. Also, just like the Bible foretold, we have recently seen Jews returning home to Israel in great numbers. So much so, that not long ago (1948) Israel officially became a nation again - also just like the Bible predicted it would--after centuries of being unrecognized as such (Deuteronomy 30:3-5)!

The great Old Testament prophet Daniel predicted much about the last days and the end times. For example, in Daniel 12 he describes how **"...there will be a time of distress such as not happened from the beginning of nations until then."** And he foretold of a great surge in man's knowledge near the end, saying, **"Many will go here and there to increase knowledge."** Well, today, in our busy world, knowledge is indeed seen as the key to success--both for individuals and for businesses. People are sure going "here and there" in pursuit of knowledge--even into outer space. Scientists say we have learned more in the last 25 years than in all of recorded history combined! Isn't it fair to say that the Bible prophets certainly accurately predicted this surge in knowledge?

And, who could say that the world is not in the greatest "distress" it has ever seen? Mankind's great increase in knowledge certainly has not been able to relieve the runaway anxiety and turmoil in the world today.

From 2 Timothy 4:1-5 and many other places in the Bible, we are told that when Jesus returns, he will return as "Judge" of all mankind. Here, Paul's written instructions to his friend Timothy appear also to be a *prophecy based* wake-up call to all people living in the last days: **"In the presence of Christ Jesus, who will judge the living and the dead, and in view of his appearing and his kingdom, I give you this charge: Preach the Word; be prepared in season and out of season; correct, rebuke and encourage-- with great patience and careful instruction. For the time will come when men will not put up with sound advice. Instead, to suit their own desires, they will gather around them a great number of teachers to say what their itching ears want to hear. They will turn their ears away from the truth and turn aside to myths. But you, keep your head in all situations, endure hardship, do the work of an evangelist, discharge all the duties of your ministry."**

Speaking about watching prophesied events of the world for his return, Jesus said, **"So you also, when you see all these things, know that it is near, at the very doors."** And Jesus cautions us, **"But of that day and hour no one knows, no, not even the angels of heaven, but my Father only."** And Jesus says, **"Therefore you**

also be ready, for the Son of Man is coming at an hour when you do not expect him." These verses are also from Matthew 24.

Jesus and other Bible prophets such as Daniel, Ezekiel, Isaiah, and Jeremiah foretold all these things we've looked at so far--and much more. Their written prophecies are clear and simple, and surely not vague. You know, Jesus said in Matthew 4:4, **"Man does not live on bread alone, but on every word that comes from the mouth of God."**

Here's one more thought for us to consider before going on to the next chapter: After seeing some of the amazing Bible prophecies that have come true, and continue to come true, I can understand how a believing Christian might be able to have a certain peace of mind in this troubled world. And, perhaps these Christians are not lying when they say they look forward to Jesus' return (his Second Coming).

Chapter 18
"As it Was in the Days of Noah"

Jesus foretold, **"As it was in the days of Noah, so it will be at the coming of the Son of Man. For in the days before the flood, people were eating and drinking, marrying and giving in marriage, up to the day Noah entered the ark; and they knew nothing about what would happen until the flood came and took them all away. That is how it will be at the coming of the Son of Man"** (Matthew 24:37-41 and Luke 17).

The Bible records that Noah tried for 120 years to persuade people to repent of their wicked ways and live according to the will of God. He warned them of the great flood to come. But the people ignored Noah. Christian teachers say the Bible is warning us today (in these end times) that just like in the days of Noah, most people are ignoring God as they carry on their busy lives.

Could these Christian teachers be right? Can you see "the days of Noah" all around you? Worldly pleasures and getting material things (stuff) sure seem to be the focal point of most people's lives. Immoral and sinful living has become so common that few things are considered wrong or sinful anymore.

And today isn't it obvious that many people's hearts seem to be **"turning cold,"** just as Jesus foretold in Matthew 24:10-12? So many people don't take the time anymore to be nice to each other.

Moreover, in recent years many people have turned away from organized religion, and quit going to church, just as Jesus foretold in Matthew 24:10." Studies show that today only 8% of North American Christians regularly attend church! In the 1940's over 50% attended church regularly. This downward trend is continuing.

I know a number of people, who claim to be Christian, that are obviously ignoring the moral standards they were taught from the Bible. I've done the same thing myself, in the past. So many seem to not want to be inconvenienced or bothered by the teachings of the Bible, so they disregard the Bible and quit on church. Mark Twain put it like this:

> "Most people are bothered by those passages
> in Scripture which they cannot understand.
> The Scripture which bothers me the most
> is the Scripture I do understand."

Let us not forget that Jesus also accurately prophesied how Christians would be "hated by all nations because of him" (Matthew 24:9). Now, Christians everywhere are mocked and called "foolish" and "intolerant" of other people's religious or spiritual beliefs. Jesus also said Christians would even be hated in their own families! Jesus said, **"...A man's enemies will be the members of his own household"** (Matthew 10:34-37).

Remember, we saw in Chapter 17 that the Bible says when Jesus Christ does return, he will return as 'judge' of everyone who is alive or has ever lived (2 Timothy 4:1)! And, Jesus warned that on the day of his return many who are alive will be unprepared; and for them it will be a dreadful day with **"weeping and gnashing of teeth"** (Matthew 24:50-51). But, also in Matthew 24, Jesus said that the day of his return will be a great day for his **"faithful and wise servants,"** and he will reward them abundantly.

We here a lot of talk these days about who this Jesus Christ really was. He claimed to be the Son of God! Don't you agree with me that if a person wants to make sure they get their eternity right, it would be make sense for them to explore and consider *who* Jesus Christ really was, or is?

Chapter 19
The End of History

The old Bible sure appears to have accurately foretold how the world would be today! And, as part of our reasoning about God, religion, and reaching heaven, let's consider the fact that the Bible also gives us a detailed accounting of how the end of history will play out. I know of no other sacred book, of any other religion, that even comes close to the Bible in this regard.

Incredibly, the Bible goes beyond the "last days" prophecies and what today's Christians call the "end times" prophecies--leading right up to Jesus' Second Coming. The Bible predicts specific monumental events marking the end of the existing world, and so much more!

The Bible describes a terrible tribulation period just before Jesus' Second Coming, the rise and fall of the antichrist, the gathering up of Jesus' faithful believers in the heavens, (Christians call this the "Rapture"), the "Second Coming" of Jesus, God's rebuilding of Jerusalem (the "new Jerusalem"), Satan's last desperate battle with God (the "battle of Armageddon"), God's casting down of Satan into hell for all eternity, the creation of the "new earth" and "new heavens" by God, the thousand year reign of Jesus Christ on the new earth ("the millennium"), the resurrection of the bodies of every human being who has ever lived, the "final judgment" before the throne of God, and the entering of all human beings into their final destination of either heaven or hell for all eternity!

These are *some* of the "end of history" events that the Bible describes in detail. I must tell you, because of all the already fulfilled Bible prophecies I know of, and those I see happening around me every day, I can't help believing that every word of the Bible's predicted "end of history" will come true.

Chapter 20
The Greatest Scientist of All Time!

I have read the Bible all the way through. Being an engineer, I naturally paid close attention to those Bible verses and passages that pertain to science. I'm amazed that the writers of the Bible wrote boldly and accurately about scientific things, even though these writers lived centuries before the related scientific discoveries!

From what I've been taught about science and the laws of physics, I see nothing but sound science in the Bible. I don't recall reading a single verse in the *old* Bible that contradicts any scientific facts I know.

There are numerous examples of sound science in the Bible. Here's just a few, with their Bible reference(s). If you were to read the Bible, you would see these and many other in their full context, and likely be even more impressed.

* Ball shaped earth. Isaiah 40:22.

* Earth suspended in space. Job 26:7.

* Innumerable stars. Genesis 15:5.

* Springs and fountains in the sea. 2 Samuel 22:16.

* The hydrologic cycle on the earth. Job 26:8, Psalms 135:7, Ecclesiastes 1:6-7.

* Sickness related to sanitary conditions. Genesis 17:9-14, Leviticus 12-14.

* Knowledge of the human bloodstream--life in the blood. Leviticus 17:11.

* The Second Law of Thermodynamics related to energy conservation. Psalms 102:26, Romans 8:18-23, Hebrews 1:10-12.

Can there be any doubt about it? God is the greatest Scientist of all time! God invented science! Doesn't it seem reasonable to think that God could have inspired the writers of the Bible to include scientific facts so we would have yet another demonstration (like the prophecies) that the Bible is inspired by him, and is therefore totally accurate and trustworthy?

My favorite science related verse is Job 26:7, which says, "...**He suspends the earth over nothing**". That is just too cool!

Chapter 21
The Bible Says it is "God Breathed"

We saw in Chapter 12 that the Bible itself claims to be inspired by God. I can tell you, with total certainty, there are many Bible passages that make that claim--probably hundreds of them. The most known such passage is where Paul writes in 2 Timothy 3:16, **"All scripture is God breathed, and is useful for teaching, rebuking, correcting, and training in righteousness, so that the man of God may be thoroughly equipped for every good work".**

The Bible does not say God inspired some of its scripture, or most of it. As we consider the Bible, we need to remember that the Bible plainly says *all* of it is inspired by God.

Now, if the Bible is inspired by God, and presuming God does not lie or make mistakes, we are compelled to consider this profoundly important reasoning thought: We know that many people who claim to be Christian say they believe the Bible, but they also say they honestly can't believe certain parts of the Bible. But if the things they don't believe are actually true, can their disbelief make these *true* things untrue? Of course it cannot. Truth is always truth, isn't it? It's like this: If I believed with all my heart that 2+2 is 4, 4+4 is 8, and 8+8 is 27, would that make 8+8 = 27? Think about it.

This simple truth is *all* the Bible is true, or none of it is true! Isn't it totally unreasonable and silly to grade the Bible "on a curve"? If the Bible is inspired by God, then it simply must be error free and totally trustworthy; otherwise, what good is any of it? You know, the implications of this simple reasoning sure seem very serious for those who claim to be Christian, or are considering becoming one.

Chapter 22
The Eyewitnesses

Both today's historians and the writers of Jesus' day generally acknowledge that Jesus Christ existed and that his twelve apostles were usually with him during his ministry (about three years)-- leading up to his death by crucifixion. History shows that these twelve apostles and Paul wrote most of the New Testament within 35 to 60 years after the death and resurrection of Jesus. The apostle John wrote that Jesus said he was God; and he wrote that he saw Jesus prove he was God by his many miracles, especially Jesus' own resurrection! Jesus told the apostles, **"...believe the miracles, that you may know and understand that the Father is in me, and I in the Father"** (John 10:38). And in John 10:30, Jesus boldly says, **"I and the Father are one."** (In Chapter 29 we'll look at other important Bible verses that show precisely who Jesus was, and is).

History records that many early Christians were rounded up and fed to the lions in the Roman coliseum. They would be placed inside the skin of sheep and put before the lions! Obviously these early Christians must have stood out and held firm to their belief that Jesus Christ is the Lord God. Why were these early Christian martyrs so steadfast in their faith? More than likely, many of these Christians were eyewitnesses to one or more of Jesus' miracles and also heard him teach.

History also records that most of the apostles were tortured and killed because they persistently kept spreading the news about Jesus and his miracles that they witnessed first hand. If these apostles were lying about seeing Jesus' many miracles and about seeing and talking with the *risen* Jesus, then we have to ask ourselves this question: Why would they knowingly risk being murdered by spending their lives spreading the news about Jesus Christ and his teachings?

The resurrection of Jesus Christ is the foundation of the Christian faith. Without the resurrection, the things the Bible teaches about reaching heaven would be of no real consequence, would they?

Let's consider this: The enemies of Jesus Christ surely would have loved to disprove his resurrection, by producing his dead body. I (and many much smarter people than me) doubt that Christianity would be around today if anyone had been able to find Jesus' dead body. But once Jesus was resurrected, his dead body was no longer anywhere to be found! And the Bible describes how the apostles John and Peter looked into Jesus' empty tomb and **"believed"** the resurrection because Jesus' burial linens were still intact where his body was laid. To John and Peter, it must have looked like Jesus had vaporized (John 19:39-40 and 20:7-8)!

You know, it seems logical to expect that the apostles would have been nearby when Jesus was crucified. Their New Testament writings tell us they saw him, talked with him, and even ate with him *after* his resurrection. As we saw in Chapter 15, Paul assures us that the *risen* Jesus appeared to the apostles and others on various occasions. In 1 Corinthians 15:6, Paul seems quite excited as he recounts Jesus' appearance to a crowd of some 500 people!

From all this, we surmise that until Jesus returns to earth, as he promised, no one can *prove* beyond a shadow of doubt that his resurrection occurred. Of course, no one can prove the resurrection did not happen, can they? Nevertheless, there sure is a lot of evidence for the resurrection--from what we know *about* and *from* the Bible, and even from recorded secular history. There is considerable 'factual' and 'logical reasoning' evidence for the resurrection. You and I have only looked at a very small portion of this evidence. Isn't it fair to say that belief in the resurrection does not have to be totally based on faith?

Could it be that the creator God knows what's best for us, and having *some* faith in the resurrection of Jesus Christ is something we all need for our own good?

The Twelve Apostles of Jesus Christ (from Matthew 10) **are:**

Simon, who is called Peter
Andrew, his brother
James, *the son* of Zebedee
John, his brother
Philip
Bartholomew

Thomas
Matthew, the publican
James, *the son* of Alphaeus
Lebbaeus, whose surname was Thaddaeus
Simon, the Canaanite
Judas Iscariot

Chapter 23
How Much Faith is Needed?

The New Testament shows that many people in Jesus' day saw his miracles and believed him to be the world's long awaited Savior. And, we learn in Acts that after Jesus' resurrection the Christian church grew rapidly in numbers--as many people came to believe - without seeing Jesus and his miracles! We should also consider that as the early Christian church grew, the New Testament had not yet been written, and only a very few people had hand written copies of 'portions' of the Old Testament. So, people generally could only listen as others told stories from the Old Testament, and told about Jesus miracles and teachings. So, obviously considerable faith was required in these early days to believe in Jesus Christ and the things he said regarding heaven and hell--and how to reach heaven.

We can make a good case that it takes less faith now to believe Jesus Christ is the Savior than it did in the early days after his resurrection. That's because today we have a much more vivid awareness of God's vast creation--including ourselves, all forms of life, and the universe. And we have the full written Bible!

As you no doubt have already surmised, I am a believer in Jesus Christ. Because of everything you and I have reasoned about up to this point, I believe. I know in my heart that I have gotten my eternity right. Sure, it takes some faith for me to believe, but I don't consider that it takes too much faith. God has given me plenty enough to see, without being an eyewitness to Jesus.

The things we will consider, as you and I finish up our reasoning journey in this book, have helped to strengthen my belief. Maybe they will help you to believe, or strengthen your belief, if you already believe. Either way, I think you will find that the final leg of our journey was the best part of it!

Chapter 24
About Going to Heaven

Jesus Christ affirms to us, **"I am the way, and the truth, and the life. No one comes to the Father except through me"** (John 14:6). And Jesus tells us of his Father's love for all people: **"For God so loved the world that he gave his one and only son, that whoever believes in him shall not perish but have eternal life"** (John 3:16).

Does God desire that we go to heaven? The Bible tells us over and over that God loves all people, and wants none of us to miss out on heaven. One such verse is 2 Peter 3:9, which says, **"The Lord is not slow in keeping his promise, as some understand slowness. He is patient with you, not wanting anyone to perish, but everyone to come to repentance."** It is abundantly clear from the Bible that no one has ever been born that God did not *want* to reach heaven.

Regarding reaching heaven, here's a crucial truth the Bible teaches: The Bible makes it abundantly clear, in many places, that merely proclaiming Jesus' name does not guarantee one's salvation! Jesus puts it this way: **"Not everyone who says to me, 'Lord, Lord' will enter the kingdom of heaven, but only he who does the will of my Father who is in heaven"** (Matthew 7:21).

So, what does God want from you and me, and everyone? Does the Bible show us a specific, unmistakable way - God's way - to reach heaven? Is there a way to know for sure that we have gotten our eternity right? Yes indeed! God's Bible tells us *precisely* how we can have our eternal salvation secured and never loose it!

Chapter 25
Heavenly Thoughts

Here are *some* of the things God promises in his Bible for those who reach heaven. I call these "heavenly thoughts."

Speaking of heaven, Paul tells us, **"No eye has seen, no ear has heard, no mind has conceived what God has prepared for those who love him"** (1 Corinthians 2:9).

Here are some 'heaven' promises from the Bible:

* God the Father, the Lord Jesus Christ (God's Son), and the Holy Spirit will be there (Daniel 7:9, Revelation 4:2-3, 5:6, 7:17, 14:13, Hebrews 1:1-3, Luke 24:51, John 20:17).
* There shall be no sin in heaven (Revelation 21:27).
* Heaven is beautiful--like a glorious city of pure gold and precious gems (Revelation 21:11,18; Psalms 52:2).
* The river of life will be there to insure everlasting life (Revelation 22:1).
* Heaven is a place of perfect holiness (Revelation 21:27).
* Heaven is a place of great joy (Psalms 16:11).
* Those in heaven will sing with joy (Isaiah 44:23, Hebrews 2:12).
* Heaven is a never ending place (John 3:15).
* There are no tears in heaven (Revelation 7:17, 21:4).
* Sickness is not allowed there (Revelation 22:2).
* No pain is allowed there (Revelation 21:4).
* There is no death there (Isaiah 25:8, 1 Corinthians 15:26, Revelation 21:4).
* There is no hunger or thirst there (Revelation 7:16).
* Heaven has no night (Revelation 21:25, 22:5).
* Angels will be there (Daniel 7:10, Hebrews 12:22).
* We will have a recognizable body in heaven (1 Corinthians 3:2).

* Our heavenly body will be like Jesus' "glorious" resurrected body (Philippians 3:21, 1 John 3:2).
* We will eat in heaven (Luke 24:41-43, John 21:12-13).
* We will learn in heaven (1 Corinthians 13:9-10).
* We will serve in heaven (Revelation 7:15, 22:3).

I can only anticipate that heaven will be a place of unimaginable joy. I'm sure the Creator of the universe can take care of us in heaven--just as he promises us in the Bible.

Revelation 21:4 assures us, **"He will wipe away every tear from their eyes. There will be no more death or mourning or crying or pain, for the old order of things has passed away."**

Chapter 26
Hell is a Real Place

Jesus Christ warned us more about hell than he talked about heaven. If the Bible is the word of the one true God, then hell is a real place. And, unless Jesus Christ was a liar and a fraud, then hell is a real place. In Chapter 29 we will see why Jesus truly does have authority to speak about the place hell.

The Bible says hell never ends and people there can never be freed from it. Remember, we saw earlier that God loves us all and he wants none of us to end up in hell. Jesus' apostle Peter tells us in 2 Peter 3:9, **"He is patient with you, not wanting anyone to perish, but everyone to come to repentance."**

And the Bible very clearly cautions us, time and again, that when we die our course is set; there is no opportunity to repent after death. That's God's rule. Hebrews 9:27 states it like this: **"Just as man is destined to die once, and after that to face judgment."** There is no mention in the Bible of any after-death restitution or rehabilitation. Here are some Bible descriptions of hell:

* Hell is eternal sorrow with weeping and gnashing of teeth (Matthew 8:12).
* Hell is a place of remorse (Luke 19-31).
* Hell is where frustration and anger abound (Matthew 13:42, 24:51).
* Hell is a place of misery and pain without rest (Revelation 14:10-11).
* Hell lasts for all eternity (Daniel 12:2, Matthew 25:46).

In Matthew 18:9, Jesus warns, **"And if your eye causes you to sin, gouge it out and throw it away. It is better for you to enter life with one eye than to have two eyes and be thrown into the fire of hell."**

Chapter 27
Do Good People Go to Heaven?

From cover to cover the Bible clearly shows us that none of us even remotely deserves heaven! We could look at hundreds of passages supporting this truth. Romans 3:23 says this to us: **"For all have sinned, and fall short of the glory of God."** Isaiah 6:3 says, **"Holy, holy, holy is the Lord Almighty."** The Bible also teaches us in many places that God is holy *and* just; and that God says death is the only just punishment for sin. Romans 6:23 says, **"For the wages of sin is death."**

Romans 5:12 shows us, **"Therefore, just as sin entered the world through one man** (Adam)**, and death through sin, and in this way death came to all men, because all sinned--for before the law was given, sin was in the world."** Isaiah 59:2 reminds us, **"But your iniquities have separated you from your God; your sins have hidden His face from you,..."**

And, no matter how good and moral we think we are, we cannot hide our sins from God--sins such as those little lies, gluttony, envy, jealousy, stealing little things, impure thoughts or deeds, cheating, lusting, taking God's name in vain, gossip, and on and on! And we all sin by omission. Sins of omission are the things God commands us to do, that we choose not to do. The Bible clearly defines all sin.

We know from the Bible that we all should humbly admit we are guilty sinners who fall far short of God's glory. The Bible tells us this very plainly in numerous passages. 1 John 1:8 says: **"If we claim to be without sin, we deceive ourselves and the truth is not in us."**

Yes, all of us are naturally sinful. We all have free will; and we all choose sin regularly. And the devil is always looking for ways to tempt us into sinning. Even in the Garden of Eden, the devil successfully temped Adam and Eve to sin against God. Mankind has been sinning ever since.

Nevertheless, many people let pride conceal their sin from them.

Their pride deceives them. Pride tells them they are basically good because they do good things for others and because they don't do really bad things to anyone. So sure, compared to the generally violent and treacherous world we live in, it's easy to think we're pretty good. But, we need to understand that what really counts is how we compare to God--and his commands to us; and on that score card we are all batting zero! None of us deserves to be in God's holy presence--just like Romans 3:23 says.

Even the great man of God, Moses, was a dreadful sinner and was not deserving of being in God's presence. We see in the Old Testament that God spoke aloud to Moses many times, but Moses was not permitted to get close to God or see his face. Once, when Moses was about to walk up close to God, God warned him, **"Do not come any closer, ...for the place where you are standing is holy ground"** (Exodus 3:5). Likewise, in our sin condition we are not fit to be with God in heaven! Maybe it's as if any sin in heaven would pollute heaven like a drop of poison in a glass of water. In any case, isn't it reasonable from all this to conclude that only one's foolish pride could trick a person into thinking they're good enough for heaven?

Over and over, the Bible assures us that how good and moral a life we lead has nothing to do with reaching heaven; because in this life we can never be good enough to be free of sin.

Chapter 28
Can We Earn Our Way to Heaven?

We've seen that no one deserves heaven, and being good won't get anyone there. Then, does God expect us to earn our way to heaven, perhaps by works or deeds? The Bible gives us God's answer in Ephesians 2:8-9, **"For it is by grace you have been saved, through faith--and this is not from yourselves, it is the gift of God--not by works, so that no one can boast."**

Many people hope that doing good works will at least improve their chances of reaching heaven. And a number of religions teach that we *earn* our way to heaven by our moral living and doing good works, including being baptized. These ideas are not in the Bible!

In the New Testament, we see that people were only baptized *after* they accepted Jesus Christ as their Lord and Savior. The Bible shows us that baptism by water is a valuable inward confirmation and public demonstration of one's *conscious decision* to put their faith in Jesus Christ. Perhaps that's why nowhere in the Bible is the baptism of a baby or child ever specifically mentioned. The Bible shows us in Acts that it was a tradition that new believers got baptized. But, nowhere does the Bible tell us that anyone is saved through baptism, or even becomes a Christian through baptism! It is significant that Jesus never baptized, his disciples did (John 4). Even so, Jesus did teach us to baptize new believers (Matthew 28:19-20). Jesus certainly did not need to be baptized, but he allowed John the Baptist to baptize him (Matthew 3:12-16).

The great baptizer, John the Baptist, said that he baptized with water, but that Jesus Christ would baptize by the Holy Spirit (John 1:33, Mark 1:8). This gives us a great insight into how we are actually saved by Jesus Christ *with* the Holy Spirit, and not saved by water baptism done by another person, even by such a great person as John the Baptist. In summary, by considering *all* the Bible, it would seem most reasonable to conclude that when *we* baptize a person, that is a very good thing, but it is certainly *not* the saving thing.

All this does not mean that doing good works or deeds is not worthwhile. In Matthew 22:36-39, Jesus commands us, **"Love your neighbor as yourself."** There are numerous Bible verses telling us we ought to do good works. But, like being baptized, when we examine the Bible regarding *how* we reach heaven, we just don't find passages that tell us good works, in themselves, can get us to heaven. Good works is not the way.

Nevertheless, the Bible consistently tells us that once our salvation is taken care of, we can then **"store up"** rewards in heaven by our good works--provided we do these good works because we treasure God. I like that.

Jesus said, **"Do not store up for yourselves treasures on earth, where moth and rust destroy, and where thieves break in and steal. But store up for yourselves treasures in heaven, where moth and rust do not destroy, and where thieves do not break in and steal. For where your treasure is, there your heart will be also"** (Matthew 6:19-21).

Remember, nowhere in the Bible is it recorded that Jesus said anything like, do good works and you will be saved.

So, we can reason from God's word that *his* way to heaven is not based on our good works, our job, our church membership, our education, or our baptism. This is a crucial truth that really matters. We can't earn our way to heaven--period. So, is there any hope for us sinners? Yes! God, through his goodness, grace, mercy and love for us, provides the way. And we know that his way is the only way because he says so through his Bible.

Chapter 29
Jesus Christ

Most everyone has heard the saying "Jesus saves." That saying is so true; but there is much more that we need to know. Exactly who is Jesus Christ? Why does Jesus Christ have authority to save anybody? How does he save us? Are there other ways to be saved, perhaps by another name? Does the creator God have a plan that he is following in all of this?

From the Bible, we find the answers to all these questions. First, we know that God has a plan for us. Second, we clearly can see what his plan is. And third, the Bible assures us that his plan works because he is God and he can accomplish whatever he chooses. He made the universe didn't he? Revelation 4:11 reminds us, **"You are worthy, our Lord and God, to receive glory and honor and power, for you created all things, and by your will they were created and have their being."** And Jeremiah 29:11 tells us, **"For I know the plans I have for you," declares the Lord, "plans to prosper you and not to harm you, plans to give you hope and a future."**

Remember, we saw earlier that we are all sinners; and we are separated from our Creator by our sin. In Genesis 3, we learn that Adam committed the first sin; and we learn that sin spread from Adam to all mankind (Romans 3:23, 5:12). Isaiah 59:2 also tells us, **"Your iniquities have separated you from your God; your sins have hidden his face from you."** Also, as we saw earlier, Romans 6:23 tells us that we are condemned to death by our sin. It says, **"For the wages of sin is death."**

But, by the Bible, we know God's plan for this lost world was to send his only Son, Jesus Christ, into the world to save us from that "death" of eternal punishment for our sins. Jesus' sacrificial death *for us,* and his resurrection from the grave three days later, gives us the *opportunity* to be forgiven and not have to endure eternity separated from God. Jesus' resurrection affirms his power over death. It shows us that *only* Jesus Christ is Lord and Savior who gives eternal life.

Recall what Jesus said in John 3:16: **"For God so loved the world that He gave His only begotten Son, that whoever believes in Him shall not perish but have eternal life."** And Romans 5:8 says, **"But God demonstrated his own love for us in this: While we were yet sinners, Christ died for us."**

The Bible shows us that, on his own accord, Jesus fulfilled his Father's plan of salvation for us. Jesus said before his crucifixion, **"I lay down my life--only to take it up again. No one takes it from me, but I lay it down of my own accord. I have authority to lay it down and authority to take it up again. This command I received from my Father"** (John 10:17b-18).

The writer of Hebrews describes Jesus Christ's power and authority to be the Savior of the world. Hebrews 1:1-3 teaches us, **"In the past God spoke to our forefathers through the prophets at many times and in various ways, but in these last days he has spoken to us by his Son, whom he appointed heir of all things, and through whom he made the universe. The Son is the radiance of God's glory and the exact representation of his being, sustaining all things by his powerful word. After he had provided purification for sins, he sat down at the right hand of the Majesty in heaven."** The Bible shows us that Jesus Christ is the Son of God; and he is equal to God the Father, and equal to God the Holy Spirit. Today, Christians call this the "Trinity." They refer to Jesus as the "second person of the Trinity." In chapter 33 we will learn how the Bible shows us crucial truths about 'who God is'.

Here's one of my favorite Bible verses: Jesus Christ proclaims to us, **"I am the way, and the truth, and the life. No one comes to the Father except through me"** (John 14:6). And, Acts 4:12 assures all people that Jesus Christ is the *only* way to salvation: **"Salvation is found in no one else, for there is no other name under heaven given to men by which we must be saved."**

In 1 Corinthians 8:6, the Bible says, **"There is but one Lord, Jesus Christ, through whom all things came and through whom we live."** And many times Jesus clearly demonstrated that he is the Lord God by his many miracles, especially his resurrection. Jesus says to us, **"I and the Father are one"** (John 5:19-25). And Jesus said, **"I am the resurrection and the life. He who believes in Me, though he may die, he shall live. And whoever lives and believes in Me shall never die. Do you believe this?"** (John 11: 25-26).

From these verses, and many other Bible passages, it is apparent that the Bible clearly teaches that Jesus Christ was, and is God!

I'm saddened when I hear people say they just cannot accept that Jesus Christ was anything more than a good man and another great moral teacher. The renowned Christian writer, C.S. Lewis, replies to such talk in his book, *Mere Christianity*, where he says:

> "A man who was merely a man and said the sort of things Jesus said wouldn't be a great moral teacher. He'd either be a lunatic–on a level with a man who says he's a poached egg–or else he'd be the devil of hell. You must make your choice. Either this man was, and is, the Son of God: or else a madman or something worse. But, don't let us come with any patronizing nonsense about his being a great human teacher. He hasn't left that open to us. He didn't intend to."
>
> **C.S. Lewis**

Chapter 30
Get Saved

Here it is: God's Bible tells us that to be saved, and thereby reach heaven, we need to **"believe"** that Jesus Christ is Lord - the God who was born a man so he could *allow* himself to be tortured and killed as punishment for our sins, and then rise again after three days. And, we need to **"repent"** of our sins. Doing these things is *free,* and that's how we saw (Chapter 28) God's word describe our salvation as **"the gift of God"** in Ephesians 2:8-9.

Romans 10:9-10 says, **"That if you confess with your mouth, "Jesus is Lord," and believe in your heart that God raised him from the dead, you will be saved. For it is with your heart that you believe and are justified, and it is with your mouth that you confess and are saved."**

Remember, Jesus tells us we must also repent. Jesus says, **"Unless you repent, you will all likewise perish"** (Luke 13:3).

It is shown over and over in the Bible that those who *believe* and *repent* are saved; and God sends his Holy Spirit to dwell inside those new saved believers! Ephesians 1:13-14 declares, **"And you also were included in Christ when you heard the word of truth, the gospel of your salvation. Having believed, you were marked in him with a seal, the promised Holy Spirit, who is a deposit guaranteeing our inheritance until the redemption of those who are God's possession--to the praise of his glory."**

Jesus also said that those who *sincerely* believe and repent are **"born again."** Jesus plainly said, **"I tell you the truth, no one can see the kingdom of God unless he is born again"** (John 3:5).

The apostle John shows us in his gospel (John 3) how Jesus goes on to explain that being "born again" is not a physical rebirth, but is a rebirth by the Holy Spirit of God--as the Holy Spirit brings us from spiritual death to spiritual life! In John 3:5-8, Jesus teaches, **"Flesh gives birth to flesh, but the Spirit gives birth to spirit."**

Think about that for a moment. Paul says the new believer is a

"new creation." He says in 2 Corinthians 5:17, **"Therefore if anyone is in Christ, he is a new creation; the old has gone, the new has come"**! And Paul reminds those who have been born again, **"Your body is a temple of the Holy Spirit who is in you, whom you have received from God,..."** (1 Corinthians 6:19).

So, a person gets saved, or gets "born again" like Jesus describes, when he or she humbles their self in a *sincere*, personal prayer to God. In this prayer a person tells God, in their own words, that they *believe* his Son, Jesus Christ, died on the cross as penalty for their sins; they believe Jesus rose again after three days in the grave; and they accept Jesus as their Lord and Savior. They ask God to forgive their sins, and they *repent."* They promise God that from now on they will try to do his will by following the will of his Son, Jesus. They ask God to send his Holy Spirit to be with them--to guide them for the rest of their life. This is the way God gives us to show him that we accept his free gift of eternal salvation with him in heaven.

Praying this prayer marks a defining moment in one's life, and changes them forever! God's word clearly teaches that the very moment one sincerely prays this prayer their eternal salvation is secured and they become a true born again, saved Christian. They have gotten their eternity right!

Today Christians call this prayer the "sinner's prayer," or "prayer of repentance." People praying such a prayer may feel inadequate and clumsy in their words, but they can be assured that God sees their *sincere* heart. The Bible says, **"The Lord does not look at the things man looks at. Man looks at the outward appearance, but the Lord looks at the heart"** (1 Samuel 16:7).

Sure, faith and humility are required in sincerely praying to get saved--and becoming a Christian. Proud people can have great difficulty accepting God's *gift* of salvation, because they tend to have great difficulty recognizing their sin and their true position in the cosmos relative to God's position. James 4:10 encourages us, **"Humble yourselves before the Lord, and he will lift you up."** Salvation is a gift from God, but salvation is not a right, and salvation is not automatic!

The Bible tells us in Acts 11:26 that the first people to be called Christians were the believers of Jesus Christ who lived in the city of Antioch along the east shore of the "Great Sea" (Mediterranean Sea).

It is clear from the Bible that only born again people can legitimately be called Christian. Nevertheless, there are many people today claiming to be Christian who have never been born again.

Remember, God tells us we must believe *and* repent to be born again saved. To repent simply means that we are sorry to God for our sins; and we resolve, by his grace, to try with all our might to turn from sin. People who have sincerely repented do not d*eliberately* sin anymore! The apostle James reminds us not to depend merely on believing, when he says, **"You believe that there is one God. Good! Even the demons believe that--and shutter"** (James 2:19). Hebrews 10:26-27 says, **"If we deliberately keep on sinning after we have received the knowledge of the truth, no sacrifice for sins is left, but only a fearful expectation of judgment and of raging fire that will consume the enemies of God."**

Chapter 31
The Best Deal Ever!

One morning in 1994, *by God's grace*, I humbled myself and prayed to God with all my heart for my salvation. I told God I believed in his son Jesus Christ and I repented of my sins. I believe God answered my prayer as I was praying it! I felt his Holy Spirit come to me, and I wept with joy. He saved me right then! I was born again saved; and by the grace of God I had just become a true Christian. I was a "new creation" in Christ by that rebirth! It was the greatest day of my life!

Now, I can tell you I have felt God's Holy Spirit with me ever since--just as the Bible promises. By the Holy Spirit, God is my *personal* and best friend! And by that friendship I receive all God's abundant promises for my life--promises he offers believers in his Bible. What a great deal - the best deal ever! Now, *with God's help,* I'm trying to be a faithful follower of Jesus Christ. And my life has a certain peace and purpose now, because God's Holy Spirit is with me and I know for certain I have gotten my eternity right!

Here's another great thing about being born again. God promises us that once we've been saved by becoming born again, we can never be separated from his love. We can never loose our salvation! And there are many Bible passages assuring us of this truth. One of my favorites is where Paul tells us in Romans 8:35-39, **"...for I am convinced that neither death nor life, neither angels nor demons, neither height nor depth, nor anything else in all creation, will be able to separate us from the love of God that is in Christ Jesus our Lord."**

And in Romans 8:28, God makes another wonderful promise to all who are saved. Romans 8:28 says, **"And we know that in all things God works for the good of those who love him, who have been called according to his purpose."** I can testify in behalf of this promise. I've seen it come true for me so many times that I now feel comforted in the midst of troubles, because I know God *always* makes things even better for me in the long run! Romans 8:28 is a special Bible verse for me. It always helps me to ponder over this verse, and I love to tell other people about it.

Isn't it a reasonable observation that in the world today there are many false teachings about how to get saved? In these "last days" many people are falling victim to *man-made* religions and futile *man-made* ways to their salvation--just as the Bible foretold and warned us long ago. God gives us *his* way to reach heaven. His way is the *only* way, and it is the only way we need! Remember, God does not want us to fail to get saved because of our pride. Proverbs 16:18 warns, **"Pride goes before destruction, a haughty spirit before a fall."**

You know, when we try to rationalize God's plan of salvation, we can't make sense of it. In all our reasoning, it is the one thing that defies all logic. The *way* he chose to free us of our sin debt seems totally illogical to us. How can the all-powerful eternal God, who created the universe, love us so much that he would take on the form of a human being - and then allow himself to be killed so that we might live? For God to become a man is as if you or I would willingly become a worm--for the good of the other worms! We mere human beings simply cannot rationalize God's plan of salvation. Thankfully, all he wants us to do is accept it - and use it.

So, I urge you, be humble, believe and repent. Get born again saved! Eternity is worth getting right. You don't have to go forward in a church to be saved. There is nothing in the Bible that says we even need to be in a church building when we pray for our salvation. We can't be too far from God to be heard, and we can't be in too much sin to be forgiven.

Chapter 32
Dandy Daydreams

Ever since I got saved and got my eternity right, I am not the same person I once was. I'm no longer imprisoned by the desires of this world. My mind is free to daydream about things that really matter. I often daydream about heaven and what it will be like to have a body that never gets sick and will never grow old and die. I ponder about how awesome it will be to live forever in heaven. Hardly a day goes by that I don't think about 1 Corinthians 2:9 which tells us we can't even imagine how great heaven will be! I daydream about hanging out in heaven with my golfing buddies; and I wonder if there will be games in heaven that will be even more fun than golf. I often daydream about meeting Jesus and his apostles-- and all the great people of God from the Bible. I can't wait to listen to their stories!

I wonder what God will do with the universe - will it be an endless playground and workplace for those in heaven? Billy Graham once said he believes that.

I daydream and think about such things all the time. But, there is one thing I'm really concerned about. I'm concerned for all the people around me, my closest relatives, and people all over the world, who do not have dandy, 'positive' daydreams about heaven, because they are troubled in the heart about their prospects for even reaching heaven. I was in that place for much of my life. That's why I couldn't help writing *Eternity Is Worth Getting Right*. Jesus said in Matthew 7 that the road to heaven is **"narrow"** and **"only a few find it."**

Chapter 33
Who God Is--the Trinity

Most people have heard of the Trinity, but few know what the Trinity is--in regard to the Christian faith. The Trinity is at the heart of the Christian faith, for it tells us who God is; and it is supported by the entire teaching of scripture in the Bible.

God tells us who he is by showing us his nature in the Bible, and "Trinity" is the name Christians use to describe his *revealed* nature. Webster's dictionary defines trinity as "a set of three persons or things that describe a unit." The Bible explains that God is three distinct persons in one nature or being. The Bible says these persons are the Father, the Son, and the Holy Spirit, who exist as the one true and living God. So, in Christian teaching God is called a triune God or Trinity.

Of course, we do not understand how there are three distinct persons in the one God since there is nothing like it in our human experience. It is reasonable to admit that we mere human beings will never totally understand God's *divine* triune nature. Only God could tell us who he is in a way that we could even partially understand his nature--or who he is.

God reveals his triune nature to us in a clear and orderly *progression* through the Bible. From Genesis through Revelation, we see that the Father, the Son, and the Holy Spirit were together as *one* God in the beginning; that none of them were created--they always existed; and they will always be together in the *one* God for all eternity!

God's revealing begins in Genesis 1:1 which says, **"In the beginning God made the heavens and the earth."** This shows us that God the Father is the one who desired to make the universe, and he is the one who is forever in charge of it. We also know this from many other Bible passages, such as Revelation 4:11, which says, **"You are worthy, our Lord and our God, to receive glory and honor and power, for you created all things, and by your will they were created and have their being."** In Matthew 24:36 Jesus points out that *only* the Father in heaven knows when the end of the world will come. Jesus says, **"No one knows about that day or hour, not even the angels in heaven, nor the Son, but only the Father."** The Father is in charge of everything.

In Genesis 1:26, God the Father says to the Son and to the Holy Spirit, **"Let Us make man in Our image, according to Our likeness;..."** Genesis goes on to show us that they all worked *together,* as one, in creation.

In the Old Testament we see God the Father speaking aloud to people such as Adam and Eve, Abraham, Moses, Jacob, Noah, Job, the ancient prophets, and others. It is interesting that God the Father never allowed anyone to see him face to face, because, as He told Moses in Exodus 33:20, **"You cannot see my face; for no one may see my face and live."**

And in the Old Testament, God shows us how the Holy Spirit is *active* doing many works of the Father. Genesis 1:2 shows us that the Holy Spirit has always existed and was the *agent of creation* along with the Father and the Son. Genesis 1:2 says, **"Now the earth was formless and empty, darkness was over the surface of the deep, and the Spirit of God was hovering over the waters."**

Here's a couple more Old Testament passages showing the Holy Spirit working with God the Father: In Ezekiel 37:1 we learn that the Holy Spirit lifted the prophet Ezekiel up in the air and moved him from one place to another. And Ezekiel 36:27 tells us that God the Father told Ezekiel that he would send his Holy Spirit to his chosen people to help them keep his laws. Ezekiel writes that God says to the Israelites, **"And I will put my Spirit in you and move you to follow my decrees and be careful to keep my laws."** We'll look at more Holy Spirit *actions* in a moment.

And then in the New Testament, God's triune nature is revealed to us much more vividly when God the Father sends his Son Jesus into the world. Jesus' visible life on earth clearly demonstrates that God's infinite power and authority is shared *equally* between the Father, the Son, and the Holy Spirit! From the Bible's recordings of Jesus' teaching, preaching, and performing miracles, we learn a great deal about God's triune nature. Throughout his ministry, Jesus never fails to tell us that he accomplishes the works given to him by his Father, *only by the oneness and equality of being* that he shares between his Father and the Holy Spirit.

Here are a few more Bible passages that show the triune nature of God. You know, God has provided that the description of his triune nature is completely harmonious throughout the Bible.

We know the Bible often refers to the Son, who became Jesus of Nazareth, as **"the Word"** (ex. Revelation 19:13). John 1:1-3 and 14 tells us, **"In the beginning was the Word, and the Word was with God, and the Word was God. Through him all things were made; without him nothing was made that has been made...The Word became flesh and made his dwelling among us."** So we see here that "the Word," who became the incarnate God-man Jesus, was with God the Father in the beginning; *was* God in the beginning; and took on human flesh when he came into the world to save it. And this passage also shows us that the Son, or Word, made the earth and the universe by authority from the Father.

And John 17 shows us that God the Father gives many works to his Son Jesus and the Holy Spirit to do--and the authority to do them. In John 17:4-5, Jesus acknowledges to the Father, **"I have brought you glory on earth by completing the work you gave me to do. And now, my Father, glorify me in your presence with the glory I had with you before the world began."** John 14:1-4 shows us that Jesus also prepared heaven. Before Jesus ascended into heaven, he said to his apostles, in John 14:1-4, **"I am going there to prepare a place for you..."**

In Matthew 28:18, Jesus said to his disciples, **"All authority in heaven and on earth has been given to me. Therefore go and baptize them in the name of the Father and of the Son and of the Holy Spirit."** Note here, Jesus did not say "baptize them in the *names* of..."; rather, Jesus was saying go baptize them in the *single name* of God--who is the Father, the Son, and the Holy Spirit!

1 Corinthians 8:6 reminds us, **"...there is but one God, the Father, from whom all things came and for whom we live; and there is but one Lord, Jesus Christ, through whom all things came and through whom we live."**

And Hebrews 1:8 assures us that the Father knows the Son as God; it says, **"But about the Son he says, "Your throne, O God, will last forever and ever...".**

Recall from our Chapter 29, we saw some of the Bible's teaching that Jesus Christ is Lord. Repeating, Jesus said, **"Anyone who has seen me has seen the Father"** (John 14:9). And in John 10:30, Jesus said, **"I and the Father are one."**

In addition, remember we saw in John 10:17-18 that Jesus laid down his life, and had authority from the Father to take it up again! Jesus says in John 10:17-18, **"I lay down my life…no one takes it from me…I lay it down of my own accord. I have authority to lay it down and authority to take it up again. This command I received from my Father."** And we learn in 1 Peter 3:18 that the power of the Holy Spirit *within him* enabled Jesus' body to be regenerated into his new "glorified" body and be resurrected. And it is the Holy Spirit who was in Jesus as he went and preached! 1 Peter 3:18 says, **"He was put to death in the body but made alive by the Spirit, through whom he also went and preached …"**

You know, the Bible gives us hundreds of such passages demonstrating that the Father, Son, and Holy Spirit have always reigned together as one being; that they are each *equally* worthy of praise honor and glory; and that they are *equal agents of action* in the wondrous works accomplished by the one God!

A few such passages demonstrating this equality are: Genesis 1:1-3, Isaiah 48:16 and 63:9-10, John 14:16-18, Acts 5:3-4 and 9:31, Romans 8:9-11, Ephesians 2:18, 1 Corinthians 12:4-6, 2 Corinthians 13:14, and Revelation 2:7 and 11.

No less than 89 times in the Bible, the Holy Spirit is identified as Lord, holy and equal to the Father and the Son!

And recall from our Chapter 30 that God the Father sends his Holy Spirit to dwell inside all those who decide to believe and repent. To reiterate, Ephesians 1:13-14 promises Christians, **"Having believed, you were marked in him with a seal, the promised Holy Spirit, who is a deposit guaranteeing our inheritance until the redemption of those who are God's possession--to the praise of his glory."** So, *true* Christians, because of the triune nature of God, are right when they say they have the Lord Jesus, or God, or the Holy Spirit in their heart--just as God's Bible teaches.

We also see the triune nature of God, the Trinity, when we look at passages in scripture pertaining to prayer and worship. For example, in Matthew 6:9-13 the Lord Jesus, *who made the universe,* teaches us to pray to the Father in heaven. Jesus says, **"This then is how you should pray: "Our Father in heaven, hallowed be your name, your kingdom come, your will be done…"**

And we are taught in the Bible that only God has authority to forgive sins. The people of the Old Testament and of Jesus' day understood this truth. On many occasions Jesus Christ told repentant sinners that he forgave their sins. Because of the triune nature of God, it is perfectly harmonious for Jesus to forgive sins because he is the Lord himself--as he proved.

Here are a few more scripture references showing more of God's power and nature displayed by the Holy Spirit:

* By the Holy Spirit, God is everywhere and knows all things (Psalm 139).
* By the Holy Spirit, God searches the minds of people--he knows our heart (1 Corinthians 2:10).
* By the Holy Spirit, God inspired the writers of the Bible (2 Samuel 23:2, Isaiah 59:21, 1 Corinthians 14:37, and 1 Thessalonians 4:15). Also, this is how we see in 2 Timothy 3:16 that **"All scripture is God breathed..."**
* By the Holy Spirit, God helps believers to speak rightly about him in this lost world (Mark 13:11).
* By the Holy Spirit, God empowered Jesus and his apostles to perform miracles (1 Corinthians 12:28).
* By the Holy Spirit, God imparts the love of Christ to his believers (Romans 5:5).
* By the Holy Spirit, God stirs the minds of unbelievers (John 16:7- 11).
* And by the Holy Spirit, God will raise the bodies of believers who are deceased. Romans 8:11 says to *true* Christians, **"And if the Spirit of him who raised Jesus from the dead is living in you, he who raised Christ from the dead will also give life to your mortal bodies through his Spirit, who lives in you."**

Now, please permit me to get especially serious for a moment. The triune nature of God, the Trinity, is one of the most important and most thoroughly demonstrated truths in the Bible! A religion or belief that does not recognize and accept this truth is very likely to miss other crucial truths in the Bible--such as how we get saved! And, it's sad to say, but such a religion or belief can go by many names, but according to the word of God, cannot legitimately be called Christian.

I really like how the apostle John ties the Trinity doctrine together for us in 1 John 4:13-16. He says, **"We know that we live in him and he in us, because he has given us his Spirit. And we have seen and testify that the Father has sent his Son to be the Savior of the world. If anyone acknowledges that Jesus is the Son of God, God lives in him and he in God. And so we know and rely on the love God has for us."**

Because of God's great love for us and his revealing of himself to us in the Bible, we have the following definition of the Trinity, as described by today's Bible scholars:

> "There is but one only living and true God. There are three persons in the Godhead - Father, Son, and Holy Spirit. And these three persons are one true eternal God, the same in substance, equal in power and glory, although distinguished by their personal properties. The Scriptures manifest that the Son and Holy Spirit are God equal with the Father, ascribing unto them such names, attributes, works, and worship as are proper to God only."

Chapter 34
God's Greatest Commandment

In Matthew 22:36-39, a Pharisee expert in the law of the Old Testament asks Jesus, **"Teacher, which is the greatest commandment in the law? Jesus replied: "Love the Lord your God with all your heart and with all your soul and with all your mind. This is the first and greatest commandment. And the second is like it, 'Love your neighbor as yourself'."**

And, in John 21:15, Jesus asks the apostle Peter, **"Simon, son of John, do you truly love me more than these?" "Yes Lord", he said to him, "You know that I love you." Jesus said, "Feed my lambs."** You see, Jesus wanted Peter to know and understand that he *first* needed to love the Lord Jesus; and then, loving his neighbor would be the result of that first love.

The Lord Jesus commands us to love him. And he shows us that we can't love God without also loving our neighbor. So simple, yet who chooses to do it? True born again Christians do good works-- trying to love their neighbor. Because they love and treasure God, they *want* to do his will.

Nevertheless, there are many moral people who claim to be good Christians, but have never submitted their life to Jesus Christ by being born again. They may be a member of a church--and may even be baptized. They do good works. But they do not know Jesus Christ, so they cannot love him. They do not have the Holy Spirit of God in them. According to the word of God they simply are not true Christians at all. Speaking of such people, Jesus says, in Matthew 7:21-23, that on judgment day he **"...will tell them plainly, I never knew you. Away from me, you evildoers!"**

Jesus says in Matthew 6:21, **"For where your treasure is, there your heart will be also."** Are we good and kind to others simply because it's "nice to be nice," or because we first love God with all our heart, soul, and mind? God sees our heart. God knows what we truly treasure? God cannot be fooled, and he cannot be bribed!

Loving God should be our highest priority in life. Here are two great Bible verses to remember and live by: Jesus said, **"Whoever finds his life will lose it, and whoever loses his life for my sake will find it"** (Matthew 10:39). And Jesus asks, **"What good will it be for a man if he gains the whole world yet forfeits his soul?"** (Matthew 16:26).

Saint Agustin said, "Love God with all your heart, and sin all you want." You see, Saint Agustin realized that if we truly love God, we are compelled to hate our sin and will fight against it with all our might!

Chapter 35
Self Help or God's Help?

The Bible says in Genesis 1:26 that God made us in his image. We look something like him. And the Bible assures us in John 3:16-17, and countless other places, that God loves us and he knows what's best for us.

Meanwhile, bookstores are running over with "self help" books, aren't they? They sell. Authors of these books are all over television promoting their books and their "great" new recipes for happiness. And still, millions of people are stressed out, angry, depressed, and over medicated. It doesn't make any sense does it? Something is bad wrong. And it's getting worse all the time.

Here's my point: I expect that God is saddened because so many people do not use his word, the Bible, as their first source of wisdom. They judge the Bible as irrelevant without ever opening it up and looking inside. They have no idea what great help they're missing. In my view, the Bible has more wise counsel, that works, than all the self help books ever written--put together!

Proverbs 3:6 says, **"In all your ways acknowledge him, and he will make your paths straight."** By the Bible, God offers us *all* the most important counsel we could ever need in life--from managing money, to marriage success, to getting along with our neighbor, to taking care of our bodies and our minds, to finding true inner peace and joy, to growing old gracefully, and - best of all - to getting our eternity right!

Joshua 1:8 teaches us, **"Do not let this Book of the Law depart from your mouth; meditate on it day and night, so that you may be careful to do everything written in it. Then you will be prosperous and successful."** The prosperity Joshua refers to has little to do with worldly possessions.

Chapter 36
Going to Church

In the Old Testament (Exodus), we learn that God, through Moses, gave his people (the Israelites) very detailed instructions on the setting up of regular worship services. God commanded them to come together to worship him; and he promised to be there when they did, to hear their prayers and accept their offerings. So they regularly worshiped God together in their "Tent of Meeting," which was an elaborate tent that they moved from place to place with them in the desert.

Then, in the New Testament, we see that Jesus grew up going to the synagogue (church) every Sabbath day (the Lord's Day), where Old Testament scripture was taught and preaching was done. As a youth Jesus studied the scriptures. The Bible says that young Jesus amazed the people at the synagogue, especially the elders, with his knowledge of scripture. (The scripture at that time was the writings of the Old Testament. The New Testament would be written a few decades later--after Jesus' death and resurrection). And though Jesus Christ was God in the flesh, the Bible tells us he was also totally human. He had to eat and sleep; and like any other person, he got fatigued at times and had to rest. And he needed to study to learn those scriptures he quoted so often.

On the instruction of Jesus, the apostles spent their lives starting Christian churches; and they taught others how to worship God, and how to keep their church upright and faithful.

There are many Bible passages relating the importance of going to church for all those who love God and his son Jesus Christ. Hebrews 10:25 instructs us: **"Let us not give up meeting together, as some are in the habit of doing, but let us encourage one another-- and all the more as you see the day approaching."** The "day approaching" the writer speaks of here is Jesus' Second Coming.

And Jesus promises, **"For where two or three come together in my name, there I am with them."** (Matthew 18:20).

A true born again Christian who has given his life over to the will of Jesus Christ *wants* to be in church every week. And, they want to read their Bible and pray to God often. If you're contriving excuses in your mind for not going to church, then perhaps you are supporting a divide between you and the God who created the universe--a divide that he does not like or condone!

The third commandment of God, handed down to us through Moses, says we must **"Remember the Sabbath day by keeping it holy."** That's obviously not a request or suggestion. And, we've already seen that God's greatest and most important commandment is to love him with all our heart, soul, and mind. I ask you, in light of all these things, how can anyone seriously claim to be a true Christian and not even *want* to make an effort to attend church every week? Nevertheless, only God is our judge - only God can see into a person's heart.

Before Jesus ascended into heaven after his resurrection, he left all Christians with a great task. Today's Christians call this task "Jesus' great commission." Jesus directs his church in Matthew 28:19-20, **"Therefore, go and make disciples of all nations, baptizing them in the name of the Father and of the Son and of the Holy Spirit, and teaching them to obey everything I have commanded you. And surely I am with you always, to the very end of the age."**

One of the neat benefits of becoming a born again Christian is that going to church becomes something you want to do. And believe me, attending a faithful church makes all the difference in the world. Truly faithful churches are almost always exciting and busy places that provide fuel for one's soul. They are the opposite of boring!

There are many good faithful pastors heading up many good faithful churches. Appendix 2 gives you a good insight into how to find the right church home.

Chapter 37
Difficult Bible Verses

Indeed, there are difficult or hard to understand verses in the Bible, particularly in the Old Testament. Many people say they reject the Bible, and reject Jesus Christ, because of Bible verses they think show God to be cruel and unfair. For example, they point to the wrath of God when he caused the "great flood" and when he destroyed the cities of Sodom and Gomorrah. Some, who know more of the Bible, cannot accept that in Leviticus Chapter 19 God instructs Moses to use the death penalty for persons caught in certain immoral acts!

I want to be totally up front with you here. As a new immature Christian, I accepted difficult Bible verses on faith that God had an eternal plan for mankind and he was fulfilling his plan--in his way. So I didn't concern myself too much with difficult Bible verses. Now, after listening to and talking with some great Bible scholars, and reading on the subject, I feel a little better prepared to reason with you about difficult Bible verses. I know I still have much more to learn about this. But I have been taught enough that I now know I was right as a new and less informed Christian to accept the difficult Bible verses, and also right to want to know more about why I should accept them. Let's look at five points of reasoning I've been taught since becoming a Christian which serve to ease my mind on the subject. Read these and see if they help you.

POINT #1. Many people just don't take the time to learn the full context of the difficult verse(s), so of course they're more likely to see an incomplete or wrong interpretation. In order to arrive at a fair and realistic meaning of some verses in the Bible, we need to examine more verses elsewhere in the Bible that pertain to the same topic of the verse(s) in question. That's simply looking at all the related data to arrive at the proper meaning--a reasonable thing to do.

POINT #2. If we can reason that the Bible is the true word of God, then he must have had a purpose for inspiring *all* the verses in the Bible. God surely knew that some verses and passages would be troublesome for some people; and he knew that such verses would be used by skeptics to ridicule and reject the Bible.

POINT #3. I believe it's true, that most people who read the entire Old Testament in a fair-minded way, come away with the profound realization that no matter how low man sinks into sin and rebels against God, God still never gives up on mankind! Ancient peoples repeatedly demonstrated a total disdain toward God, no matter how much he did for them. For example, in the Bible we see that God, through his servant Moses, freed the Israelites from their Egyptian captives; and then the Israelites went right back to worshipping idols that they crafted with their own hands! They arrogantly abandoned God, turning to all sorts of immorality and corruption. The Bible tells us about mankind's *repeated* rebellions against God--all the way back to Adam and Eve. The more I've learned about the corrupt peoples of the ancient world, the more I understand that God had every reason, and every right, to remove all mankind from existence forever--but he did not!

POINT #4. Yes, sometimes God chooses to do things that we don't understand. But we must *humbly* remember he is the sovereign creator God who does as he pleases. And he sees all things in ways we cannot because he knows all things--past and future; and he has his own plans to fulfill. Psalm 33:11 reminds us, **"But the plans of the Lord stand firm forever, the purposes of his heart through all generations."**

POINT #5. In evaluating God's actions toward mankind, we are obliged to consider God's overall true relationship to us guilty sinners. Consider the great good that God has done for all of us. Here's a neat analogy shown me by a good Christian friend: He said, "God is like a judge in his robe sitting at his judgment bench, and we are the accused felons (sinners). He hears the evidence against us; and because he is a *just* God, he pronounces us guilty and sentences us to death. Then incredibly, this same God-Judge takes off his robe, walks around to our side of the bench and says to us, "I will become a man, and I will take the punishment for all your sins by dying in your place"! And he did, by the death of his Son, Jesus Christ, on the cross!

Near death on the cross, Jesus was heard saying, **"My God, my God, why have you forsaken me?"** (Mark 15:34).

Indeed, the Bible reveals that God is a just and wrathful God. But, it also reveals him to be a supremely merciful and loving God whom we do not deserve. This is what we need to remember. And the more one learns from the Bible, as they mature in their faith, the more they see and appreciate the goodness of God.

Chapter 38
Be Encouraged

Suppose for a moment, that you choose to believe, and you accept Jesus Christ as your Lord and Savior. You are sincerely sorry to God for your sins; you ask God to forgive you; and you truly repent by *trying* to stop sinning. You've been "born again." You're a "new creation," a new Christian! Then perhaps, as an outward sign of your new personal relationship with God and your new membership into the Christian faith, you get baptized--or re-baptized. (I got re-baptized at the age of 49. I was first baptized as an infant).

Then, no matter how long you honestly try, you just can't conquer some habitual sin in your life. Maybe for you, overcoming this sin seems like an impossible mountain to climb! I sin in various ways every day; and I'm still fighting against a particular sin that has been with me for as long as I can remember. I pray often to God for his help in conquering all my sins.

I think we all need to keep in mind a few truths about sin--truths that are abundantly clear from the Bible. We know from the Bible that the only person to ever live their life free of sin was Jesus Christ. Even the Pope sins everyday. Mother Theresa was a sinner--just as you and I.

We all are sinners. But God knows your heart, and mine. God knows whether or not we are *sincerely* trying to stop sinning. Completing a total turnaround to become sin free is utterly impossible for all of us. There will always be sins for us to battle no matter how many sins we may conquer. And nowhere does the Bible distinguish between a serious sin and a so-called minor sin. We know from God's word that *all* sins are serious!

Remember, the Bible teaches us, **"... for all have sinned and fall short of the glory of God"** (Romans 3:23). However, because of Jesus Christ's sacrificial death on the cross and his resurrection from the dead, there is hope for us sinners. God's great love for us gives us the *opportunity* to have our sins forgiven and be saved.

Also, Jesus says to you and me, **"In this world you will have troubles, but take heart, I have overcome the world"** (John 16:33). Sometimes it seems as though life is just one troubling thing after another, doesn't it? But here, and in numerous other passages, Jesus reminds his believers that because of him we can have true joy now and in the next life! I like John 10:10, where Jesus says, **"I came that they may have life, and have it more abundantly."**

Here's one of the most amazing and encouraging things I've ever learned from the Bible: Before Jesus left the world he prayed to his Father in heaven for Christians! We read Jesus' prayer in John 17:9-26. Jesus Christ, *who made the universe*, prayed, **"I will remain in the world no longer, but they are still in the world, and I am coming to you. Holy Father, protect them by the power of your name--the name you gave me--so that they may be one as we are one...I say these things while I am still in the world so they may have the full measure of my joy within them. I have given them your word and the world has hated them, for they are not of the world any more than I am of the world. My prayer is not that you take them out of the world but that you protect them from the evil one..."**

Here's another encouraging thing you should know. When and if you choose to enter into a personal relationship with Jesus Christ by being born again, you will receive *personal* help and protection from God's holy angels. Hebrews 1:14 shows us: **"Are not all angels ministering spirits sent to serve those who will inherit salvation."**

Chapter 39
The True Meaning of Life

Think back to the first few chapters of this book relating to creation and the sovereignty of God. Think again about your true position in the cosmos - God's cosmos.

As you and I near the end of our reasoning journey, I humbly share with you this common man's definition of the true meaning of life:

> "To me, the true meaning of life is: God gives us our time here in this life so we can freely choose to '*believe*' that Jesus Christ is Lord and Savior; and we can freely '*repent*' of our sins, assuring our salvation with Him in heaven. Then, for the rest of our present life we love the Lord Jesus and try to do his will that he shows us in the Bible. And we watch and pray for opportunities to tell others how we were saved, so they too might choose to get saved."

Chapter 40
The Old Ecuadorian Lady

In June of 2005 I went on a mission trip to Ecuador with members of my home church at the time--Ninth and O Baptist Church in Louisville, Kentucky. One evening there, I preached on the truth of the Bible and how we can get saved.

Just after the service ended an old Ecuadorian lady, with tearful eyes, approached me and said (through one of our interpreters) "I look forward to seeing you in heaven someday Patrick (Patricio)."

I will remember that dear sweet old lady for the rest of my life; and I look forward to seeing her in heaven someday. Maybe, by the grace of God, she had just believed and repented. I don't know. She just seemed to be totally content; and I had a strong sense that those tears in her eyes were tears of joy because she knew in her heart she was saved. And I remember thinking at that moment, how could anyone have more joy in this world than that?

Please consider these Bible verses which are reserved for born again Christians who have gotten their eternity right:

"Praise be to the God and Father of our Lord Jesus Christ! In his great mercy he has given us new birth into a living hope through the resurrection of Jesus Christ from the dead, and into an inheritance that can never perish, spoil or fade--kept in heaven for you, who through faith are shielded by God's power until the coming of the salvation that is ready to be revealed in the last time...Though you have not seen him, you love him; and even though you do not see him now, you believe in him and are filled with an inexpressible and glorious joy, for you are receiving the goal of your faith, the salvation of your souls" (1 Peter 1:3-9).

Well, that brings us to the end of our journey. I hope you liked it; and I hope and pray that, if you haven't already done so, you begin right away your journey with the Lord Jesus Christ. That's the journey that really matters most. It begins with your prayer of belief and repentance, and continues along the road to eternal heaven. If you are, at best, only curious about Christianity and Jesus Christ, then I most humbly suggest three things to you: First this curiosity may very well be God's Holy Spirit speaking to your heart. Second, I suggest you pray to God about it. And third, I urge you to read the gospel of John in the New Testament. May God bless you.

The end.

ACKNOWLEDGMENTS

Most importantly, I want to publicly thank Lord Jesus for answering my prayers by providing me with so much support and encouragement from so many people as I wrote this book. It is only by his grace that I was able to finish. I love you Father God.

I'm grateful to my beautiful wife, Jeannie, because she rescued me countless times from my weak computer abilities. Her patience to keep supporting and assisting me through this project demonstrates her unfailing love for me. Thank you so much sweetheart.

Mother and daddy have always shown interest in my book. They read my first few drafts and gave me useful feedback. And they listened carefully, like loving parents do, as I talked of my dreams and plans for this book. Thank you so much, both of you. I love you.

Finally, I'm so thankful to my dear friends at Ninth and O Baptist Church in Louisville--my home church at the time of this writing. I might have given up on this project were it not for all their loyal encouragement and sound advice. I want to recognize Dr. T. J. Betts, Larry Buchanan, Dr. Jeff Elieff, Ted Kantorski, Jim Meeks, Blake Ring, Dr. David Sills, and Dr. Steve Wellum. I'm especially pleased to brag on Dr. Wellum because he humbled himself enough to review several drafts of this book. He suggested many important improvements relevant to it being in harmony with God's word and Christian teaching. I learned so much from him and all these faithful Christians. May God bless them all, and may God continue to bless Ninth and O.

Appendix 1
God's Ten Commandments

I You shall have no other gods before me.

II You shall not misuse the name of the Lord your God.

III Remember the Sabbath day by keeping it holy.

IV Honor your father and your mother.

V You shall not murder.

VI You shall not commit adultery.

VII You shall not steal.

VIII You shall not give false testimony against your neighbor.

IX You shall not covet your neighbor's house.

X You shall not covet your neighbor's wife.

Note: The Ten Commandments are taken from Exodus 20:3-17
.

Appendix 2
Finding the Right Church Home

The most important thing in selecting your church home is to make absolutely certain you have found a *faithful* church. A faithful church is a church with faithful leaders, especially a faithful pastor. Faithful churches are where the *entire* Bible is preached and taught regularly. And the Bible message of God is not added to or subtracted from--as instructed by John in Revelation 22. Beware of pastors who mostly preach those popular feel-good sermons--while rarely mentioning sin. They may preach with great eloquence and claim to know Jesus Christ, but they have little resemblance to him in their preaching! The number of members in a church has nothing to do with whether or not it is faithful to the word of God. Remember, Jesus Christ convicted people of their sin so they would repent. Jesus Christ was crucified for the things he said and taught.

Faithful churches are busy in their neighborhoods ministering to those in need and sharing the gospel of Jesus Christ with the lost. Faithful churches are also actively involved in winning the lost of the world to Jesus by contributing to Christian world missions and by encouraging and helping their members spread Jesus' gospel to the ends of the earth.

You need to be aware that there are plenty of faithful churches; they just take more effort to distinguish than they used to. That's because today, in these "end times," there are many *unfaithful* pastors who are leading people astray by shaping and tempering their preaching to suit the preferences and life styles of a fallen world. These unfaithful pastors are nothing more than some of the false prophets that the Bible foretold would deceive many in the last days! So, I urge you to select your church with care, with prayer, and with guidance from those who know a faithful church when they see one.

Appendix 3
The Books of the Bible

GENESIS	Gen	NAHUM	Nah
EXODUS	Exod	HABAKKUK	Hab
LEVITICUS	Lev	ZEPHANIAH	Zeph
NUMBERS	Num	HAGGAI	Hag
DEUTERONOMY	Deut	ZECHARIAH	Zech
JOSHUA	Josh	MALACHI	Mal
JUDGES	Judg	MATTHEW	Matt
RUTH	Ruth	MARK	Mark
1 SAMUEL	1 Sam	LUKE	Luke
2 SAMUEL	2 Sam	JOHN	John
1 KINGS	1 Kin	ACTS	Acts
2 KINGS	2 Kin	ROMANS	Rom
1 CHRONICLES	1 Chr	1 CORINTHIANS	1 Cor
2 CHRONICLES	2 Chr	2 CORINTHIANS	2 Cor
EZRA	Ezra	GALATIANS	Gal
NEHEMIAH	Neh	EPHESIANS	Eph
ESTHER	Esth	PHILIPPIANS	Phil
JOB	Job	COLOSSIANS	Col
PSALMS	Psa	1 THESSALONIANS	1 Thes
PROVERBS	Prov	2 THESSALONIANS	2 Thes
ECCLESIASTES	Eccl	1 TIMOTHY	1 Tim
SONG OF SOLOMON	Song	2 TIMOTHY	2 Tim
ISAIAH	Isa	TITUS	Tit
JEREMIAH	Jer	PHILEMON	Phil
LAMENTATIONS	Lam	HEBREWS	Heb
EZEKIEL	Ezek	JAMES	Jam
DANIEL	Dan	1 PETER	1 Pet
HOSEA	Hos	2 PETER	2 Pet
JOEL	Joel1	JOHN	1 John
AMOS	Amos	2 JOHN	2 John
OBADIAH	Obad	3 JOHN	3 John
JONAH	Jona	JUDE	Jude
MICAH	Mica	REVELATION	Rev

Appendix 4
Bibliography

1. International Bible Society. *The Bible, New International Version (NIV)*. Grand Rapids, Michigan: The Zondervan Corporation, 2002.

2. Harbor, Frank. *Reasons For Believing.* Green Forest, AR: New Leaf Press, 1998.

3. Boyd, Gregory A. and Boyd, Edward K. *Letters From A Skeptic.* Colorado Springs, CO: Chariot Victor Publishing, 1994.

4. Hanegraaff, Hank Jr., *The Bible Answer Book.* Nashville, TN: Thomas Nelson Book Group, 2004.

5. *Precious Bible Promises.* Nashville, TN: Thomas Nelson Publishers, 1984.

6. Kaiser Jr., Walter C., Davids, Peter H., Bruce, F. F., and Brauch, Manfred T. *Hard Sayings of the Bible.* Downers Grove, IL: InterVarsity Press, 1996.

7. VanderKam, James and Flint, Peter. *The Meaning of the Dead Sea Scrolls.* New York, NY: HarperCollins Publishers, 2002.

8. Ridenour, Fritz. *So What's the Difference?* Ventura, CA: Regal Books, 2001.

9. Cheetham, Nicolas. *Universe.* London, ENG: Smith-Davies Publishing, 2005.

10. Hanks, Jr., Billy. *A Call to Joy.* Salado, TX: International Evangelism Association, 1994.

11. Graham, Billy and Lucado, Max. *God's Sacrifice for You.* Nashville, TN: Thomas Nelson, Inc., 1992.

12. Hutchings, Samuel. *Pearls of Wisdom.* New York, NY: American Tract Society, 1869.

13. Sears, Francis Weston and Zemanski, Mark W. *College Physics.* Reading, Massachusetts: Addison-Wesley Publishing Company, Inc., 1960.

14. House, Wayne H. and World of Bible Ministries. *Charts of Bible Prophecy.* Grand Rapids, MI: Zondervan, 2003.

15. Willmington, H. L. *Book of Bible Lists.* Wheaton, IL: Tyndale House Publishers, 1987.

16. Lewis, C. S. *Mere Christianity.* New York, NY: MacMillan, 1952.

17. Sills, M. David. *The Missionary Call.* Chicago IL: Moody Publishers, 2008.

18. D. A. Carson. *The Gagging of God, Christianity Confronts Pluralism.* Grand Rapids, MI: Zondervan, 1996.

19. Derek Tidball. *The Illustrated Survey of the Bible.* Minneapolis, MN: Bethany House Publishers, 2001.

20. Nelson, Thomas. *New Illustrated Bible Dictionary.* Nashville, TN: Thomas Nelson Publishers, 1995.

Notes

www.ingramcontent.com/pod-product-compliance
Lightning Source LLC
Chambersburg PA
CBHW071013040426
42443CB00007B/748